Song of Songs, Proverbs and Ecclesiastes

Song of Songs, Proverbs and Ecclesiastes

Meditations from Solomon's three books

John R. Barber

Song of Songs, Proverbs and Ecclesiastes
Meditations from Solomon's three books

Copyright © John Barber 2021 – all rights reserved

www.jrbpublications.com

Book 1 – Song of Songs: Love is strong as death
Book 2 – Proverbs: The way of wisdom
Book 3 – Ecclesiastes: Life under the sun

ISBN 978-0-9537306-7-4

First Edition: August 2021
Published by: John Barber, Southend, England

All rights reserved. No part of this publication may be reproduced, stored in a retrieval system or transmitted in any form by any means, electronic, mechanical, photocopy, recording or otherwise without prior permission of the publisher, except as provided by copyright law.

Cover design: www.greatwriting.org
Book layout and design: www.greatwriting.org

Unless noted otherwise, Scripture quotations are taken from the The Authorized (King James) Version of the Bible.

Table of Contents

General Introduction..8
About Solomon 10
Solomon's prayer of dedication of the Temple 12
About this Book..15
About the Author..17
Acknowledgements 18
Glossary 19
Outside the Camp revisited 20
The Books of Solomon in today's tumultuous times 23

Book 1: Song of Songs 26
Introducing the Song..27
Approaching the Song..29
Interpreting the Song 32
Day 1: The Song of songs (1:1)..39
Day 2: Intimate love (1:2) 40
Day 3: Black and comely (1:5) 41
Day 4: Horses and chariots (1:9)..42
Day 5: Thou art fair (1:15) 43
Day 6: The Rose of Sharon (2:1) 44
Day 7: The Apple Tree (2:3)...45
Day 8: His banner over me (2:4)..46
Day 9: Not to stir up love (2:7) 47
Day 10: Leaping upon the mountains (2:8)...........................48
Day 11: My fair one come away (2:10) 49
Day 12: Taking the little foxes (2:15).....................................50
Day 13: My beloved is mine (2:16) 51
Day 14: Lost and found (3:1) 52
Day 15: The King in his splendour (3:6)................................53
Day 16: Like a flock of goats (4:1)..54
Day 17: A heart that is ravished (4:9) 55
Day 18: A garden inclosed (4:12) 56
Day 19: North and south winds (4:16)..................................57
Day 20: Knocking at the door (5:2).......................................58
Day 21: What is thy beloved like? (5:9).................................59
Day 22: White and ruddy (5:10)..60
Day 23: Reunited (6:2)...61
Day 24: An army with banners (6:4) 62
Day 25: Like a palm tree (7:7) 63
Day 26: His desire is toward me (7:10) 64
Day 27: Like a brother (8:1)...65
Day 28: A seal upon thine heart (8:6) 66

Day 29: Many waters cannot quench love (8:7) 67
Day 30: The little sister (8:8) 68
Day 31: Make haste, my beloved (8:14) 69
Praying the Song 70
Singing the Song 72
The Song 73

Book 2: Proverbs 80
Introducing Proverbs 81
Approaching Proverbs 84
Interpreting Proverbs 86
Day 1: Fear and Wisdom (1:7) 89
Day 2: Seeking understanding (2: 3-5) 90
Day 3: Trust in the Lord (3:5,6) 91
Day 4: Guard your heart (4:23) 92
Day 5: The loving deer (5:18,19) 93
Day 6: Go to the ant (6:6) 94
Day 7: Keep God's commands (7:1) 95
Day 8: Wisdom cries out (8:1) 96
Day 9: Reprove not a scorner (9:8,9) 97
Day 10: A wise son (10:1) 98
Day 11: The liberal soul (11:25) 99
Day 12: Heaviness of heart (12:25) 100
Day 13: When to keep quiet (13:3) 101
Day 14: A way which seems right (14:12) 102
Day 15: A soft answer (15:1) 103
Day 16: Pride comes before a fall (16:18) 104
Day 17: The quiet life (17:1) 105
Day 18: The way of the fool (18:2) 106
Day 19: Concerning the poor (19:1) 107
Day 20: The pure in heart (20:9) 108
Day 21: A good leader (21:1) 109
Day 22: A good name (22:1) 110
Day 23: Buy the truth (23:23) 111
Day 24: Do not envy evil men (24:1) 112
Day 25: Be kind to your enemies (25:21,22) 113
Day 26: Dealing with fools (26:4) 114
Day 27: Not boasting of tomorrow (27:1) 115
Day 28: Righteous and wicked compared (28:1) 116
Day 29: The fear of man (29:25) 117
Day 30: God's pure word (30:5) 118
Day 31: A God-fearing woman (31:30) 119
Proving Proverbs 120

Book 3: Ecclesiastes 122
Introducing Ecclesiastes 123
Approaching Ecclesiastes... 127
Interpreting Ecclesiastes 130
Day 1: Vanity of vanities (1:3).. 135
Day 2: Nothing new under the sun (1:9).. 136
Day 3: No profit under the sun (2:11).. 137
Day 4: Eat, drink and enjoy (2:24) 138
Day 5: To everything there is a season (3:1) 139
Day 6: Discovering the works of God (3:11) 140
Day 7: Injustice in the world (3:22) 141
Day 8: The oppression of the oppressed (4:1) 142
Day 9: The quiet life (4:6) 143
Day 10 The Desirability of Companionship (4:9) 144
Day 11: Attitudes toward God (5:1) 145
Day 12: Attitudes toward money (5:10,11) 146
Day 13: Attitudes toward death (5:15,16) 147
Day 14: Content with our lot in life (6:1,2).................................... 148
Day 15: The uncertainties of life (6:12) 149
Day 16: A better way to live (7:5,8) 150
Day 17: It is back to wisdom (7:19).. 151
Day 18: The meaning of life (7:25)... 152
Day 19: Being wise is a good thing (8:1) 153
Day 20: Fearing God is a good thing (8:12,13) 154
Day 21: What we don't know (9:1)... 155
Day 22: Time and chance (9:11,12) 156
Day 23: Wisdom and foolishness contrasted (9:17,18)................... 157
Day 24: Portrait of a fool (10:1) 158
Day 25: Wise words that are gracious (10:12) 159
Day 26: Our attitude toward rulers (10:20).................................... 160
Day 27: Casting our bread upon the waters (11:1) 161
Day 28: Life is a gift (11:9,10) 162
Day 29: Remember God when you are young (12:1)...................... 163
Day 30: The conclusion of the matter (12:9-11) 164
Day 31: The whole duty of man (12:12-14) 165
Education from Ecclesiastes 166

Prophets Priests Kings and Jesus.. 169

General Introduction

Preface

The first thing to say is this preface is not about one book but, rather, three. The common factor is the author of each of the Bible books referred to in this three in one book is King Solomon, the third king of Israel (although some dispute this, and we will consider why later). The first of these books, on the Song of Songs, was written two years ago and was part of a project that began over forty years prior to that. It has undergone minor modifications to bring about a near common style and accommodate further thoughts. The other two, Proverbs and Ecclesiastes respectively, have been written more recently. They have been brought together under a single cover, as much for the sake of convenience as for marketability.

The second thing to say is this preface, like many prefaces, is meant to whet the appetite of readers, and entice would be readers. While this author believes his book(s) contains some great content, that is hardly a good enough reason for people to read the writings of someone who is not well known or has credentials that people give much store to, like being a well-known ordained minister or a big shot in a church related context, or why they should read this book when there are so many excellent books out there and we live in a day when book reading is hardly a priority for most people. The best that can be said for now is the Song of Songs, Proverbs and Ecclesiastes are three of the sixty-six books that make up the Word of God (Bible) and as such deserve to be read in their own right, and if this devotional come commentary helps achieve this, then it can be said: job done.

Often these books are much neglected (although the same could be said for much of the rest of the Bible), not well enough understood and indeed misunderstood, and lots of the treasure and beneficial stuff contained therein that is waiting to be discovered is often overlooked. This book is meant to help remedy this deficiency and maybe a gap in the market by simply presenting what is in these three Bible books, providing context and framework, attempting to make sense of some of the more challenging sections and to encourage further study. While this book is more aimed at ordinary Christians who want to understand better what Solomon had to say in his three books, it also gives significant store to sound scholarship.

Finally, and importantly, there will no doubt be some readers who wish to cut to the chase and delve straight into the daily meditations and not dwell on the pontifications of an author who by his own admission tends to go on. The advice he gives to such folk is to be his guest, delve straight in and be blessed!

About the Cover

The front cover includes the painting "Love is strong as death" by the Plymouth Brethren, Pre Raphaelite artist, John Jewell Penstone (1817-1902).

The back cover includes three (from a choice of many) images found in the Song of Solomon: vineyard (2:13), dove (2:14), rose of Sharon (2:1), together with motifs representing respectively the books of Proverbs and Ecclesiastes.

About Bible versions

The author is pro King James Version (KJV) and unless otherwise stated, when quoting from the Bible, it is from the KJV, which is the default. There are many excellent features about the KJV – the beauty and familiarity of the language and, despite some of it being archaic, it usually accurately translates the original text. A new generation may prefer one or other of the modern translations and that is fine, providing one recognises no translation precisely conveys all of the original meaning, and neither can it. Often the original Hebrew cannot be easily translated, at least word for word and, in books like those of Solomon, there is rich imagery and poetic licence that needs considering as well as the cultural context in which Solomon operated. It is difficult to do justice to what he wrote when trying to convey to contemporary audiences the meaning of what was originally intended.

The author found (often to his surprise) modern paraphrase versions like the Good News Translation (GNT) and The Message (MSG) often provided refreshing insights into what Solomon was really getting at. Other versions used include the New International Version (NIV), English Standard Version (ESV), Amplified (AMP), New King James Version (NKJV) and the New American Standard Version (NASV). Besides the matter of versions, often in attempting a clear understanding of the original text, the author has referred to commentaries and dictionaries, including classics such as those writings of Strong and Vine.

About Solomon

King Solomon was a remarkable character, not least because he authored these three books of the Bible, as well as useful and profound works we no longer get to see. It is also reckoned he authored some of the Psalms. *"Blessed be the Lord God, the God of Israel, who only doeth wondrous things. And blessed be his glorious name for ever: and let the whole earth be filled with his glory; Amen, and Amen"* Psalm 72:18,19 and *"Except the Lord build the house, they labour in vain that build it: except the Lord keep the city, the watchman waketh but in vain"* Psalm 127:1 may be two further examples of Solomon's insights and wisdom.

But for a successful counter coup, with the assistance of the likes of Nathan the prophet and Zadok the priest, responding to an attempted coup by Solomon's elder brother, Adonojah, along with his gang, to steal the throne from the one their father David had nominated to be his successor, following his death, i.e. Solomon, he might well have disappeared into oblivion because of this usurper action, instead of ruling over the kingdom of Israel that was never greater or more secure before or after Solomon's reign. Undoubtedly, God had other plans as He did when another son of David, Absalom, earlier had tried to steal the throne.

Solomon's story as king was one who began well and finished badly. When God came to Solomon in a dream at the start of his reign (1Kings 3) and asked what He could give Solomon, Solomon's response was for an understanding heart to judge his people, that he may discern between good and bad who is able to judge this people. This pleased God, who not only gave him wisdom and an understanding heart but promised him both riches, and honour too.

Arguably, the highlight of Solomon's reign was the building of the Temple, which his father, David, wanted to build and made plans and preparations for, but God did not allow it – he had too much blood on his hands for one thing. The temple showed how the worship of God was meant to be first and foremost in his reign and thereafter. In dedicating the Temple, God came down in power, and then there was Solomon's remarkable prayer and God's response to it – all fantastic stuff.

There are plenty of examples covering Solomon's reign to illustrate his wisdom and wealth. Two spring to mind – when two women came to Solomon to seek justice, each accusing the other of stealing her child, Solomon called for a sword to cut the child in half and give each woman a half. This caused the true mother to call for the other woman to have the child and was seen as an early example of his extraordinary wisdom. The other example worth citing was when the Queen of Sheba came to visit Solomon in order to check out his wisdom and wealth and after hearing first hand concerning his wisdom and seeing his wealth, she was blown away and could declare afterward that the half had not been told her and his wisdom and prosperity exceeded the reports which she had heard.

The tragedy was that Solomon drifted away from the one true God in later life, brought about in part by marrying foreign wives who brought with them their own false gods. This sowed the seeds for the division of the Kingdom and while there were highlights, especially when the reigning king was a good one, the general trajectory was downhill, culminating centuries later in Israel and later Judah both being taken into captivity. Solomon's story is much about what could have been. He had everything he could ever dream of and, while his three books were a superb legacy, his helping sow the seeds for Israel's later demise was not.

Given Solomon understood what true love was about (Song of Songs), what true wisdom was about (Proverbs) and how life without God would end up (Ecclesiastes), it is rather ironic that the one who knew all this failed to consistently apply these important principles in his own life and reign. One sobering conclusion is that we may know what is the right thing to do, including those today who read his three books of the Bible, but not act on it. Another is we can begin well and finish badly (although given the choice we might prefer that it be the other way round). Yet another lesson we can derive is that God uses imperfect humans to carry out His will, including Solomon, you and me.

Solomon's prayer of dedication of the Temple

The Bible contains the record of many wonderful prayers. The prayers of Hannah (1 Samuel 1), Hezekiah (Isaiah 37), Daniel (Daniel 9) and Nehemiah (Nehemiah 1) spring readily to mind. All these prayers were offered at a time of challenge for the person praying, where the only one who could provide the way out was the Lord himself. Added to this top drawer of prayer warriors is Solomon, when dedicating the Temple, recorded in 1 Kings 8 and 2 Chronicles 6 and following his prayer for wisdom and understanding on taking the throne of Israel, recorded in 1 Kings 3 and 2 Chronicles 1.

The context for Solomon's prayer of dedication of the Temple is a beautiful one with the glory of God falling just before his prayer and after, and God coming to Solomon telling him how he was going to answer the prayer. What is so awesome about the prayer is it contains so many elements that those of us who are not part of the Covenant God had with Israel can identify with and apply in our own situations. For the purpose of this study, all quotes will be from 2 Chronicles.

The Temple was a big deal in Jewish worship and it was the centre of Israeli life and not only for the religious. While YHWH God does not live in a box (the Ark of the Covenant – He inhabits eternity), it is where He promised His presence would reside and where people turned (and encouraged to do so) as they sought to engage with Him and seek His face. *"But will God in very deed dwell with men on the earth? behold, heaven and the heaven of heavens cannot contain thee; how much less this house which I have built!"* 6:18.

Before Solomon prayed, we read: *"So that the priests could not stand to minister by reason of the cloud: for the glory of the Lord had filled the house of God"* 5:14. And afterward: *"Now when Solomon had made an end of praying, the fire came down from heaven, and consumed the burnt offering and the sacrifices; and the glory of the Lord filled the house"* 7:1.

His prayer was full of worship to an awesome (the word hardly cuts it) and covenant keeping God (recognising covenants made both to Moses and David). *"Blessed be the Lord God of Israel, who hath with his hands fulfilled that which he spake with his mouth to my father David"* 6:4 and *"O Lord God of Israel, there is no God like thee in the heaven, nor in the earth; which keepest covenant, and shewest mercy unto thy servants, that walk before thee with all their hearts"* 6:14.

His prayer was public and full of reverence and humility. *"And he stood before the altar of the Lord in the presence of all the congregation of Israel, and spread forth his hands"* 6:12. *"Now therefore arise, O Lord God, into thy resting place, thou, and the ark of thy strength: let thy priests, O Lord God, be clothed with salvation, and let thy saints rejoice in goodness. O Lord God, turn not away the face of thine anointed: remember the mercies of David thy servant"* 6:41,42.

His prayer was one of expectancy and based on the promises God had already made, which given the nature of God, he will surely keep and especially when it comes in response to the prayers of His praying people. *"Have respect therefore to the prayer of thy servant, and to his supplication, O Lord my God, to hearken unto the cry and the prayer which thy servant prayeth before thee: That thine eyes may be open upon this house day and night, upon the place whereof thou hast said that thou wouldest put thy name there; to hearken unto the prayer which thy servant prayeth toward this place"* 6:19,20.

His prayer recognised the tendency of God's people to sin but also understood the significance of the forgiving nature of God, even if He does punish. *"Hearken therefore unto the supplications of thy servant, and of thy people Israel, which they shall make toward this place: hear thou from thy dwelling place, even from heaven; and when thou hearest, forgive"* 6:21. *"Then hear thou from heaven, and forgive the sin of thy servants, and of thy people Israel, when thou hast taught them the good way, wherein they should walk; and send rain upon thy land, which thou hast given unto thy people for an inheritance"* 6:27.

His prayer recognised God's concern for truth and justice and that the Temple is the place where this could be appropriately administered. *"If a man sin against his neighbour, and an oath be laid upon him to make him swear, and the oath come before thine altar in this house; Then hear thou from heaven, and do, and judge thy servants, by requiting the wicked, by recompensing his way upon his own head; and by justifying the righteous, by giving him according to his righteousness"* 6:22,23.

His prayer was concerned with the prayers of those who prayed after him in the Temple and combined a longing for the people's welfare and God's honour. *"Then what prayer or what supplication soever shall be made of any man, or of all thy people Israel, when every one shall know his own sore and his own grief, and shall spread forth his hands in this house: Then hear thou from heaven thy dwelling place, and forgive, and render unto every man according unto all his ways, whose heart thou knowest; (for thou only knowest the hearts of the children of men:) That they may fear thee, to walk in thy ways, so long as they live in the land which thou gavest unto our fathers"* 6:29-31.

His prayer showed concern for the foreigner, especially those that want to know God and seek His will, including a concern for their welfare and God's honour (something to consider concerning immigrants today): *"Moreover concerning the stranger, which is not of thy people Israel, but is come from a far country for thy great name's sake, and thy mighty hand, and thy stretched out arm; if they come and pray in this house; Then hear thou from the heavens, even from thy dwelling place, and do according to all that the stranger calleth to thee for; that all people of the earth may know thy name, and fear thee, as doth thy people Israel, and may know that this house which I have built is called by thy name"* 6:32,33.

His prayer was prophetic, inasmuch it had a strong inkling of what would happen when the people of God turn from the Lord in the future, including them being taken into exile but at the same time offering an escape when the people turned back to God, as indeed was to happen. *"If they sin against thee, (for there is no man which sinneth not,) and thou be angry with them, and deliver them over before their enemies, and they carry them away captives unto a land far off or near; Yet if they bethink themselves in the land whither they are carried captive, and turn and pray unto thee in the land of their captivity, saying, We have sinned, we have done amiss, and have dealt wickedly; If they return to thee with all their heart and with all their soul in the land of their captivity, whither they have carried them captives, and pray toward their land, which thou gavest unto their fathers, and toward the city which thou hast chosen, and toward the house which I have built for thy name: Then hear thou from the heavens, even from thy dwelling place, their prayer and their supplications, and maintain their cause, and forgive thy people which have sinned against thee"* 6:36-39.

Following the sacrifice, that was then being offered, being consumed by fire sent from heaven and the glory coming down and filling the Temple, there were days of joy, sacrifice and celebration by the people, and at the end, after they had dispersed and gone home, the Lord appeared again to Solomon, confirming He had heard his prayer and would do as he asked, but with it came a stern warning. While God reaffirmed the covenant made with David, which ended in the furtherance of the Davidic line until the coming of Jesus, Solomon is reminded of the dire consequences should the people break that covenant. God also confirmed the important role the Temple was to play from then onward.

Part of God's response is an often-quoted verse applied by God's people today who rightly yearn for healing of their nation and for revival. *"If my people, which are called by my name, shall humble themselves, and pray, and seek my face, and turn from their wicked ways; then will I hear from heaven, and will forgive their sin, and will heal their land. Now mine eyes shall be open, and mine ears attent unto the prayer that is made in this place. For now have I chosen and sanctified this house, that my name may be there for ever: and mine eyes and mine heart shall be there perpetually"* 7:14-16.

When reading Solomon's prayer, we are amazed at his deep worship of God and concern for the welfare of the people he was to rule over and future generations, and not forgetting the foreigner (especially considering how his life was to end). There was a desire for God's glory and a sure expectation that God will act. It serves as inspiration for us today as we approach our incomparable God.

About this Book

It was the author's dream to study as many as he could find of the well over a thousand commentaries on the Song of Songs that have been produced in the three thousand years since the Song was written (many are available still in one form or another), and to study with a fine tooth comb every word meaning and that of the many images used, and then produce his "masterpiece". It was not to be and now he is of an age when time is short and the drive to do so no longer exists. Yet the desire to share some of the riches he discovered *en route* does!

While Proverbs and Ecclesiastes did not grab in quite the same way (perhaps it should have) the same considerations could just as easily have applied, except for the fact there are far less diametrically opposed interpretations concerning the original text, compared with the Song. In mitigation though, Proverbs and especially Ecclesiastes struck me as books worth studying from an early age and I have been delving into them ever since. The challenge for the Bible student was not so much finding out about its interpretation, but rather its application, and while Solomon's day and his outlook on the world may not be the same as today, the points he made remain pertinent and strangely resonate. It has been a refreshing discovery and including thoughts on these two other books of Solomon in this book turned out to be well worth the additional effort that was needed.

If one were to use one word to encapsulate what this book is meant to be about, then the word: "commentary" came to mind, although "reflections" also could fit the bill. Later, the penny dropped that what was needed was something to aid one's daily devotions. Given all sorts, including non-believers, ponder different parts, doing something to cover the whole shebang may be a worthwhile activity.

What is presented tries to comment and reflects on nearly all the verses contained in Solomon's three books (which in fairness are not all that long) and, while it probably leaves some stones unturned, there is an attempt to recognise when this happens and, when it does, to encourage readers to do their own stone turning. Then there is the question: do we make it a learned work, more concerned with forensic analysis, or one with a devotional leaning, more concerned with lifting human spirits up to heaven? Like a lot of what the author attempts, there is a bit of both involved but on reflection he concluded he can do better by focusing on the devotional, even if at the expense of good, old fashioned Bible exegesis.

A key point about devotionals is they should draw us closer to God and inspire and encourage readers to love and serve Him. This author realised early on it was not about him (even though using "author" as opposed to "I" is somewhat unwieldy). By way of compromise, while the three main sections of this book use the first person singular in the not the devotional subsections, when it comes to daily devotions (which is, after all, the central focus of this book) the first-person singular is avoided. Often, at least in the author's experience, people who write devotionals fall into the trap (trap because it can turn people off) of resorting to personal anecdotes, pious platitudes and woolly sentimentality. He has tried to avoid doing so, helped by Solomon, who gives it to us straight, often taking us out of our comfort zones. We need encouragement but also need basic truth. The "trick" (excuse the term) is to find balance, while drawing us closer to God.

This brings us to another epiphany moment – how to discuss each of Solomon's books in a month's worth (31 days) of daily reflections, supported by sufficient preamble so readers know what is in store. One of the challenges is how to divide these three books up into 31 sections and cover as much ground as possible when doing so. Each reflection is kept to a single page, making succinctness an important pre-occupation, such that one could use these as part of one's daily quiet times. A later good idea was to include a prayer with each devotion.

When asked, "*What is more important: Prayer or Reading the Bible?*", C.H.Spurgeon answered: "*What is more important: Breathing in or Breathing out?*" – this author agrees and thus the prayer. He also recognised that if people were like him, they may well want to use it as a study aid that one might dip in and out of. It matters not; what matters is that readers get to study Solomon's three books, with their unique and related messages, still relevant 3000 years on.

About the Author

The author is an ordinary guy that loves the Bible and the God of the Bible. He has been studying it for most of his life. He lives with Jolly, his wife, and Matthew, his son, and their three cats, in Southend, England, the town where he was born seventy years ago, and has lived for much of his life. He has three degrees, none theology focused, and before "retiring" has had three careers: secondary school science teacher, computer engineer / consultant and community worker. His main community interest these days is homelessness and passing the baton to the next generation. He has a particular love for and interest in India, the country of Jolly's birth. He has belonged to a number of different churches at the low end of the market, in particular the Plymouth Brethren, and these days he joins with the Strict Baptists, although he associates with all sorts of true believers, across the board. He describes himself as a Gospel Preaching, Community Activist, Watchman on the Wall. He loves to write. A lot of his writing, including blogs, can be found on his website *jrbpublications.com*. Prior to writing this book, he wrote "*Prophets of the Bible*", and is now working on the sequel: "*Kings and Priests of the Bible*".

Acknowledgements

I have been blessed over my three score years and ten to have been exposed to many who have been a good influence on my own life, and in particular and pertinent to this work, sharing from these three books of the Bible by their deeds as well as words. Practically, I am conscious of others who have played their part writing this book, in particular in proof reading, starting with Roger Ninnis and Duncan Briant back in the early days and more recently, Una Campbell, who has given the script a thorough going over. I thank Jim Holmes for helping guiding me through the "process" and making salient comments, and with the type setting and cover design. How the final product ends up, including errors that may creep in, is my responsibility. I mention my wife, Jolly, for her patient care and helping create an environment where I can write. There are countless others throughout my life who have offered insights into Solomon's three books, not least because of lives well lived. I should also add the part played by providence – being limited because of physical disability and as a result of assorted Corona lockdown measures and given freedom to write by those around me, allowing opportunity to write a book, likely few will read, but if done for the Lord, He will bless it. I should add, I have been spoiled for choice when it comes to resources (paper, but a lot online) I could draw on. Two spring to mind: "A Pathway into the Bible" by Stuart Kimber and David Pawson's "Unlocking the Bible" video series.

Dedication

I dedicate "Song of songs" to my wife, Jolly – my own beloved.

I dedicate "Proverbs" to my son, Matthew – for just as Solomon wrote his own work, for the benefit of his own son, I have a similar thought in mind.

I dedicate "Ecclesiastes" to old dears like myself, who have been there, done that and got the tee shirt, who may be somewhat incapacitated, but love the Lord.

Glossary

The intention of the author is to define terms and acronyms before they are used, although sometimes that is not possible without making the book unwieldy. The following are some used in the book, where an explanation may help.

APOCALYPTIC is about forecasting the ultimate destiny of the world.

CHURCH: strictly "*ekklesia*" – a called-out assembly or congregation (typically of Christians), sometimes universal, but often used to depict an organisation etc.

DV: (Latin: *Deo volente*) God willing.

ECCLESIOLOGY: theology as applied to the nature and structure of the church.

ESCHATOLOGY: theology concerned with the final events of history, or the ultimate destiny of humanity.

"GOOD AND BAD": in the context, for example when describing a king, is a relative term and often relates to whether that king honoured God and did right or not.

IMO, IMHO: in my opinion; in my humble opinion

ISRAEL: when Israel is used, it usually describes God's Covenant people, although sometimes it refers to the land they were promised or have occupied.

KJV: King James Version (the main version of the Bible used in the book) – other versions occasionally used include the English Standard Version (ESV), the New International Version (NIV), the Message (MSG) and the Good News (GNT).

MESSIAH: promised deliverer of the Jewish nation prophesied in the Hebrew Bible.

NT: New Testament.

OT: Old Testament.

WISDOM: the right use or exercise of knowledge; the choice of laudable ends, and of the best means to accomplish them.

YHWH: (short for Yahweh or Jehovah) is the name often ascribed, especially in the Old Testament, to God, and is often translated as "The Lord".

Outside the Camp revisited

In April 2012, I published my book *Outside the Camp – reflections of a Community Activist*. It was the first title under the label jrbpublications. The most recent title to come under that umbrella is *Prophets of the Bible*, to be followed up in the near future (DV) by *Kings and Priests of the Bible*.

In April 2014, I produced a second edition of the book, which included a number of updates, along with four further books:

1. Spirituality and Mental Health
2. The Gay Conundrum
3. Onward and Upward
4. Theological Musings

The first two were an elaboration of two subjects that earlier had particularly interested me and were touched on in the first edition of *Outside the Camp*. The third was to include new topics related to the theme of the book and the fourth was to give a theological rationale to my community activism. Around that time, I started my website jrbpublications.com and these five books were included as electronic versions that could be freely downloaded from the website along with some of my other writings. It was around that time I became a regular blogger on all sorts of subjects (which continues to this day) and I also began to maintain a regular Facebook presence (partly in order to support my blogging).

One Internet definition of Community Activist is it is a member of a community who is voluntarily working with others from that community to achieve common aims (delivering change) – someone who takes individual action or action with others in a community, in a planned way. It also represented my third career after starting off as a secondary science school teacher and then as a software engineer, including running my own business. It is what has occupied a good deal of the last twenty years of my life and has involved a mixture of paid and voluntary positions (nowadays entirely voluntary). The idea behind the book was to tell my story, including setting the record straight so to speak.

I wanted to encourage and help the next generation of community activists based on my own experience, including as a result of making many mistakes. I also had the desire to encourage Christians to get involved in their communities and where possible to work with those of all faiths and none in order to achieve common goals. I also wanted to reach out to non-Christians based on the finding common ground principle and trying to respect a variety of different perspectives. But it is also about maintaining a balance and holding one's nerve and seeking truth. I now put on my business card I am a gospel preaching, community activist, watchman on the wall, given I am into all three and believe all three to be important.

The picture at the start of this section is the painting of the Scapegoat by the Pre-Raphaelite artist: William Holman Hunt. Another definition from the Internet is that of a scapegoat is a person who is blamed for the wrongdoings, mistakes, or faults of others, especially for reasons of expediency. The Day of Atonement is the most important holy day of the Jewish calendar, when the High Priest made an atoning sacrifice for the sins of the people, the details of which are described in Leviticus 16. This act of paying the penalty for sin brought reconciliation (a restored relationship) between the people and God. A key part of the day's proceedings was selecting two goats and the casting of lots.

The goat upon whom the lot had fallen was offered up as sacrifice and the other goat was released into the wilderness, after the sins of the people had been transferred onto it as a result of the High Priest laying hands on its head. This was referred to as the scapegoat. "*And so Jesus also suffered outside the city gate to make the people holy through his own blood. Let us, then, go to him outside the camp, bearing the disgrace he bore. For here we do not have an enduring city, but we are looking for the city that is to come*" Hebrews 13: 12-14. Jesus is our scapegoat and we are called to join him by going "outside the camp" and this is the title of my book and my community activist mantra.

It has been over seven years since I produced my second edition of the book and a lot of water has gone under the proverbial bridge and there is more wisdom I would dearly love to pass on, including the thought I may have gone full circle. I have come from a Christian background that was not keen on community activism that was not church and gospel centred, but God with His own sense of humour allowed me to get involved in set ups where many around me, including the Christians, did not see church and gospel as all that important and, if they did, these would need to bend to the prevailing cultural norms. I also learned many of the pitfalls of do-gooding and the various obstacles and agendas one encounters along the way, although doing good and acting wisely, is what we should all be doing. I now see it as possible and needed to have your proverbial cake and eat it.

Getting involved in our communities in an appropriate way is the right thing to do, and there are opportunities galore, of which helping the poor and needy are all part of what we do when we love our neighbour, as is preaching the gospel (people need to be saved, but to quote Francis of Assisi – using words if necessary) and being a watchman on the wall (warning others, especially in the light of the crazy things happening around us right now that bewilders many). The need is to maintain balance and, whatever we do, let it be to the glory of God.

Whether I get to produce a third edition of Outside the Camp remains to be seen. If I do, I will try to make it less about me and more about others and to encourage others, especially Christians, to venture outside the camp. A bit like the Preacher in Ecclesiastes, and without wanting to decry the achievements of my community activist career or disillusion those who might want to draw lessons etc., I can also see a lot of what I did and the paradigm in which I operated was vanity.

The Books of Solomon in today's tumultuous times

The Hebrew Bible (Tanakh)		
The Law	**The Prophets**	**The Writings**
Torah (Pentateuch)	Former Prophets	Poetry
Genesis	Joshua	Psalms
Exodus	Judges	Proverbs
Leviticus	Samuel (1 & 2)	Job
Numbers	Kings (1 & 2)	
Deuteronomy		Five Rolls
	Latter Prophets	Song of Songs
	Isaiah	Ruth
	Jeremiah	Lamentations
	Ezekiel	Esther
	The Twelve	Ecclesiastes
	Hosea	
	Joel	History
	Amos	Daniel
	Obadiah	Ezra-Nehemiah
	Jonah	Chronicles (1 & 2)
	Micah	
	Nahum	
	Habakkuk	
	Zephaniah	
	Haggai	
	Zechariah	
	Malachi	

The Books of Solomon (Song of Songs, Proverbs and Ecclesiastes), along with those of the Psalms and Ecclesiastes, are often referred to as Wisdom literature and are part of a section of the Hebrew Bible (Old Testament) known as the Writings, which along with the Law and the Prophets form the entire Old Testament, 39 books in total – although, in the Hebrew Bible, several of these books are combined. Together with the 27 books of the New Testament, we have what is known as the Christian Bible (66 books in total), and while the general consensus among Christians (and one accepted by this author) is that these books are divinely inspired, some would want to add to or take from the "canon".

The Apostle Peter affirms: *"for the prophecy came not in old time by the will of man: but holy men of God spake as they were moved by the Holy Ghost"* 2 Peter 1:21. As for the Apostle Paul, when he wrote that: *"All scripture is given by inspiration of God, and is profitable for doctrine, for reproof, for correction, for instruction in righteousness: That the man of God may be perfect, thoroughly furnished unto all good works"* 2 Timothy 3:16-17, it is likely he was referring to the Old Testament, and these texts provide us with good reasons why studying the OT is a good thing to do. As far as this book is concerned, if the only thing achieved is getting people to do this, then it has been well worth the effort. It is this author's view that, along with prayer, our regularly studying the scriptures should be an important part of what we do in order for us to live as God intends.

Writing this book has been done while tumultuous events have been taking place in the world, and in particular the Covid-19 "pandemic" (and as this book goes to press, we are still a long way off from seeing or knowing what the end will be) with various restrictions having been and still being brought in, supposedly in order to contain the worst effects of the "virus", and this has significantly impacted all our lives, often for the worst and in ways before all this began few could have predicted. There is a lot more going on of significance, even if the media is selective in its reporting, including a lot that is bad (albeit some that is good) and the unmasking of evil, some of which, one might venture to say, we did not realise was happening until recently, and this applies all the world over.

Part of what the author does, when he blogs, is to reflect on what is going on around him and suggest what might be appropriate responses. These considerations have also been dealt with in his most recent book **Prophets of the Bible**. Where all this will end, even in the near future, is a big question, and people have offered widely different views, ranging from the bad guys prevailing, with the ushering in of the reign of the Antichrist, to the world getting a temporary reprieve as the bad guys are brought to heel. In either case, what all right minded and expectant Christians should be longing for is spiritual revival, and, whether the way ahead of us in the short term is good or bad, we serve God regardless.

For some, speculating on these matters, especially as the truth is often hard to come by and those who we might have expected to tell us the truth – don't, has sometimes been a distraction from what truly matters, including applying some of the very lessons we are able to draw when we study the three books of Solomon. While some search for truth in suspect alternative media, ignorance is no excuse and we are called to watch and pray, including "*Thy will be done*". We are not immune from what is going on in the world, even if we turn off the TV and stop watching news outlets, including mainstream, alternative and social media (sometimes a good idea). After all, we are put here on planet earth for a purpose and what happens around us affects what we are able to do and what is most prudent for us to do. One text to help us decide on such matters is: "*He hath shewed thee, O man, what is good; and what doth the Lord require of thee, but to do justly, and to love mercy, and to walk humbly with thy God?*" Micah 6:8.

As for what those lessons are, that is what the rest of this book seeks to draw. The first thing to point out is that Satan does not want us walking in truth and will do all he can to deceive believers, and often he appears to be succeeding. Our eyes must be focused on God, and that includes what He is saying in His Word, including, for our purposes, the three books of Solomon, starting with Song of Songs and "love is strong as death". While the spotlight of the Song is on two human lovers, love can permeate all around us. After all, we are commanded to love our neighbour and just as, if not more, importantly, to love God. While the realities of life in the raw sometimes appear not to lend themselves to loving, if we make that our aim, noting what the Song has to say, it will make a difference.

Then we have Proverbs and "the way of wisdom". While we can't avoid what is difficult, challenging and unpleasant even, if we walk wisely (and Proverbs tells us how we can) we will make important decisions carrying on our journey in life. And finally, we have Ecclesiastes and "life under the sun". If ever we needed a wake-up call and reality check on how life is on planet earth, then we find it here. But it is never about cynical resignation to fate etc., but rather an encouragement that by seeing how life is if God is left out, which is the norm, we can find out how life should be when God is brought into the picture. Whether Song of Songs, Proverbs or Ecclesiastes or, come to think of it, any of the other 63 books of the Bible, we can draw helpful, needed lessons on living in today's tumultuous times.

Book 1

Song of Songs

Love is strong as death

Introducing the Song

This first of three books comprises 31 short mediations (one for each day of the month), and is on the Bible book: ***The Song of Solomon***. It can be used in one's own individual quiet time, to encompass meditating on the Bible and prayer, although it could also be read in one or more sittings or serve simply as a reference that can be used when considering this Song. Most meditations are based on a single verse in the Song, although some of the meditations will relate to more than one verse. I do so partly because context and background require it and it is all important when it comes to understanding the Bible, and partly because it is my intention at the same time to cover as much of the Song as I possibly can.

I recognise, despite being familiar with and having thought about most of these verses over many years, that all too often I am still paddling in the shallows rather than out there swimming in the deep when it comes to exploring the riches in the Word. I envisage my readership will include those who know little or nothing concerning the Song as well as those with considerable depth of insight and understanding. Just prior to penning my thoughts, I was able to experiment with members of my own church Bible study group. I asked for eight volunteers and gave each a verse from the Song (one for each chapter) and invited each one to share their thoughts on what they had read. I think none would have regarded themselves as being experts on the Song and as far as I could make out did not have strong views on what the Song was meant to be about. Yet each one provided credible and helpful thoughts, demonstrating that we can all profitably meditate, even on the more challenging scriptures.

In order to be of further assistance to those seeking to understand this sublime and mysterious book, and before embarking on these meditations, as well as in order to provide a context and framework to studying the Song, I have written two chapters. The first is titled: **"*Approaching the Song*"** and contains my own story as to why, after nearly fifty years of being fascinated by and pondering on the Song, I am now writing down these thoughts. The second is titled: **"*Interpreting the Song*"** and addresses the elephant in the room – what is it all about? Because for some/many, not knowing the answer can be a sticking point, and the Song gets neglected or misunderstood as a result, which is a pity, given the riches contained in it are for all of us to enjoy. While recognising wide variations in opinion on how to interpret the Song, I try giving, while respecting detractors, an interpretive framework, without being too dogmatic, mindful that readers, including among them those who are more holy than me and who know their Bibles well, may well see things a lot differently to me.

I add three further thoughts. ***Firstly***, I quote from the Authorized (King James) version of the Bible, not because I am hung up about KJV (believing for serious study one can/should use a variety of versions and other study aids) but it is the version I am most familiar with, is as good as the alternatives and it reads better.

Secondly, and this provides a clue to my own understanding. While I am aiming what I write for any on the spectrum between knowing nothing about the Song to those who know a lot of what is worth knowing, I do so for lovers (experienced/wonderful to inexperienced/aspiring) of the Lord. I do so with the prayer readers will love Him more dearly and know more of that love He has for His loved ones, yet not to dismiss the notion that the Song is also about sexual ethics and personal relationships.

Thirdly, I believe the Song is prophetic, even though ostensibly it is one of the few Bible books that do not contain or allude to prophecy. Its subjects are young people, yet is something older people might well reflect on and, in my experience they often do. The spontaneous energy exuded may be for us oldies something reminiscent of a long-lost youth, but we do remember what it was like, including wooing, making love to and loving the love of our lives. And not only that, we look forward to the day when we can do so again and it will be even better, for we will also be with our heavenly lover forever and can say … "*Let us be glad and rejoice, and give honour to him: for the marriage of the Lamb is come, and his wife hath made herself ready*" (Revelation 19:7).

This brings us to what the Song is about. Just as Solomon's Proverbs were about wisdom, so his Song of songs is about *love*, especially that between two lovers, including obvious physical love making, but not the soppy, sentimental sort that society seems to want to promote. The importance of love is in stark contrast to that of human vanity, the subject of another of Solomon's books: Ecclesiastes. The unique love between husband and wife is foreseen at creation: "*Therefore shall a man leave his father and his mother, and shall cleave unto his wife: and they shall be one flesh*" (Genesis 2:24) and is later likened to God's relationship with Israel (Old Testament) and Christ's relationship with the Church (New Testament). The Song incorporates both thoughts, although one doubts whether the author would have had much inkling concerning the mystery of the Church. In unravelling major themes of the Bible, we can't ignore God seeks to relate to His people in love, despite their tendency to be unfaithful, and this makes the Song of Solomon especially relevant.

I dedicate the book to lovers, especially those who suffer because of the love that is "*stronger than death*" they have for the one they are betrothed to. I sense with the escalation of persecution of Christians and Jews the world over; this book comes at an opportune time. Historically, the Song has especially been of comfort to the suffering church. Not only am I on my way out and thus keen to offer these thoughts, but I want to pass on something beautiful to those left behind, realising believers down the ages have found special comfort in the Song, and they will do so yet again. I also dedicate this book to my own beloved, my wife Jolly.

Approaching the Song

I became a Christian aged 15, partly due to the efforts of the Plymouth Brethren, and it is with the PBs (middle of the road, Open section) I have been associated for much of the time since then, although I have been around a lot, having had many encounters at most points along the ecclesiological spectrum. One of my early PB experiences was attending the traditional (as far as PBs go) Sunday morning Breaking of Bread meeting. Its focus, besides on the emblems of bread and wine, was around the atoning death of Christ. The meeting's uniqueness was brothers in fellowship could share, pertinent to this emphasis, led by the Spirit.

They did contribute, not just praying and giving out hymns but sharing verses from the Bible, maybe accompanied by a short exposition. It was then I became aware of the Song. A brother might share a verse from the Song in the context of Christ's love for His Church. Two brethren stood out: Bryn Jones and Len Ladd – both I owe a great debt to. At that time, my RE sixth form teacher, George Oliver, told us he and his wife read the Song on their honeymoon, something my wife, Jolly, and I also did years later. One amusing anecdote was when I had the opportunity to preach in one of my early trips to India, I sometimes chose a verse from the Song as my text. One day my translator failed to turn up and Jolly's dad, whose English was rudimentary at best, stepped in. We reflected afterwards that the people were blessed, having listened to not one but two sermons.

From that early age, I was hooked, and from that time on, if I had an opportunity to preach it could be on the Song although given my understanding it was more to do with the beauty of Christ rather than how to make love! If someone were to ask me for my favourite book in the Bible I might well answer: Song of Solomon. I saw in the Song my own desire and journey in getting closer to the Lord, in spite of the Song specifically saying almost nothing about God or Bible doctrine.

Over the years, I have lost count how often I preached on the Song, because like my early mentors I felt there were profound applications, and for the last twenty it was my intention to write a commentary on it. I have had three bites of the cherry, available as free downloads from my website: *jrbpublications. com*, but in each case what I wrote skirted round many details in the Song, not providing specific exposition of each verse, but rather on giving overviews and applications.

If one were to enquire: why the procrastination? I could think of several reasons but one especially stands out, besides not feeling up to the task or being taken up with other projects. My particular Obsessive Compulsive Disorder (OCD) is feeling the need to thoroughly prepare and going down various rabbit holes before letting loose to the wider world what it is I wish to share. This is of particular relevance regarding the Song of Solomon. As I discovered, there have been thousands of detailed, differing commentaries on the Song since it was written some 3000 years ago, a good many of which are still around if one cared to look.

Before writing off the majority who disagree with one's own views (an all too human tendency), it is well to ponder that many who did write loved the Lord and loved the Song for that reason. One thing is obvious (which I will discuss in the next section); there have been many different interpretations and applications, a good many of which have been contradictory. In order to get it right, one needs to understand the language and the historical and cultural context, especially when it comes to the rich imagery invoked in the Song.

While my early mentors were pretty clear as to their understanding of the Song of Solomon, I soon found out that others outside that fairly confined circle had other ideas, including subscribing (much to my surprise at the beginning) to a modern trend, which was to ditch the notion there is a deeper spiritual interpretation on the lines of the divine/human relationship and instead focus on the human love aspect. I was also to discover, with one notable exception (when I fellowshipped with the Pentecostals and one of the members gave me a book on the Song her deceased husband had written) that many churches outside the PB neglected and ignored the Song, except perhaps when it came to the matter of marriage guidance.

In the 50 years I have taken a particular interest in the Song, I have read many commentaries on it by Christians from all sections of the Church and, except for some written in most recent times, these were all solely addressing the matter of divine human love using the "love story" as illustrative of some "higher" truth. Besides PB writers, like J.N.Darby and William Kelly and those nearer to this present time: W.W.Vellacot and C.E.Hocking, these covered the Early Church Fathers like Origen, a group I refer to as medieval mystics like Bernard of Clairvaux and Julian of Norwich, Puritans like Richard Sibbes, John Owen and John Bunyan, and many others, like the Chinese church planter, Watchman Nee. Helpful commentaries that focused on the theological background rather than providing much of a devotional perspective included "The Song of Solomon" by G.Lloyd Carr (part of the Tyndale series) and "Song of Songs" by Marvin Pope (although I found the much lauded Pope rather heavy going and depressing).

Other than checking out that what I write is sound, I have not referred to other commentaries when writing the daily meditations, to avoid merely adding yet another commentary to the many that are already available. One must not ignore use and meaning of language and cultural context, and I have tried to do so. Rather, I have used the opportunity to share what the Lord has laid on my heart these past fifty years and encourage a new generation to explore further and in particular meditate on the Song. Meditation has always been an important part of the Judaeo-Christian heritage, and there are many verses in the Bible that talk about meditation, like: "*My meditation of him shall be sweet: I will be glad in the Lord*" (Psalm 104:34) and many others, *e.g.* found in the Song of Songs, do so.

The discipline of meditation does not naturally fit in with today's culture, yet is something we overlook to our cost. Christian meditation is not to be confused with New Age and eastern mysticism where the aim is to empty one of self and by this means it dangerously opens the door to the spirit world. Rather, the aim of Christian meditation is to muse, ponder, contemplate, wonder, think about, and reflect upon the character, work and word of God and commune with Him. This Song, as much as anywhere in Scripture, is fertile ground for this. My aim is to help people study the Word, rediscover this discipline and be blessed as a result.

Interpreting the Song

If the qualification needed to meditate intelligently on this Song depended on having available the correct interpretation, then by my reckoning no-one would be able to do so, since having studied the opinions offered by the good and the great down the millennia it is evident that no one has got it completely right and many have been way off the mark. Having listened to what preachers have had to say on the matter and read a lot of what has been written, I can confidently say that unless one restricts oneself to a personal echo chamber, big differences in understanding and how to apply the message, exist. Sometimes these are diametrically opposed and even laughable. For example, one commentator did so when critiquing another commentator who decided when the Lover was lying between his Beloved's two breasts, what was being referred to was the Old and New Testaments. Yet even the simplest and least learned among us can profitably meditate on this sublime Song and be blessed, as countless numbers have done down the ages, and who am I to argue that was not the intention of the Holy Spirit in the first place when inspiring the Song writer.

At this point, I could attempt to write a long treatise aimed toward providing the "right" answer when it comes to understanding the true purpose of and meaning of the Song, before ending with a handful of helpful principles to be borne in mind, yet also recognising I may end up less sure about the Song of songs than any other book in the Bible, including Revelation and Daniel, despite maybe being at least as familiar with this as with any of the other 65. The best I can come up with is to outline "problem" areas, some of the main ways the learned from many different camps have responded when it comes to the challenge of finding the correct interpretation and what I think, following years of reflecting and realising many of my early mentors were far from 100 per cent correct and none got it all.

We begin with spiritual versus literal interpretations. Coming to a view will have significant bearing on our understanding. For example, the text "*he feedeth among the lilies*" (2:16) has been plausibly taken to mean having fellowship with God's people and love making, with good people coming down on one or other view (for the record, despite my general tendency to spiritualise, and mindful that this is not the view offered by some, here I go with the physical). Explanations have been put forward why in the past those learned enough to commentate on the Song ignore the obvious, like it being a sexual metaphor, with a reason suggested that considering how thinking in the church has evolved, Greek thought has been more influential than Hebraic, but to pursue further this idea is beyond the scope here.

The impression I get studying commentaries down the ages is, except for the past 100 years, say, many commentators prior to that set little store on what on the face of it is a love story involving one (sometimes two) lovers of the girl, but rather chose to emphasise a greater and more significant story to do with Yahweh and Israel (Jewish) and Christ and the Church (or individual believer)

(Christian) and how that relationship might work out in one's own situation. Both camps try to provide justification for thinking as they do but huge variations in interpretation within both camps have left me unconvinced one way or the other. (Having two lovers – the unwanted one, the king seeking one more conquest, and the wanted one, the rustic shepherd, may solve some exegetical challenges, but creates others, and I take a view that the lover is King Solomon throughout the Song, despite knowing that the Bible account of his life almost certainly disqualifies him.)

A middle path is to recognise all schools of thought and try to combine the best: There is a human love story that involves relationship development and sexual intimacy, but also part of the rationale behind the Song's inclusion in the Bible is that not only do these things matter enormously, they also illustrate a greater relationship between the divine and the human. As far as the Old Testament goes, there are several references to do with God comparing His relationship with Israel with that of a husband and his wife. Nowhere is this more graphically illustrated than with the prophet Hosea and his unfaithful wife he was told to love regardless. We find that the YHWH is the great lover idea is an important theme throughout.

In the New Testament, not only is there the narrative of the marriage supper of the Lamb, but we find it comparing the love a husband is meant to show toward his wife with Christ and the Church: "*Husbands, love your wives, even as Christ also loved the church, and gave himself for it*" (Ephesians 5:25). My own background has exposed me more to those who spiritualise and allegorise the Song than those who emphasise the literal, physical side, and while more amenable these days to the latter view, I will not dismiss the importance of the former, and even go as far to say that it is the primary reason the Song is in the Bible, when seeking understanding and finding relevance.

Whether we take the spiritual or literal approach to interpretation, we are still faced with a formidable array of imagery, a lot of which is to do with the natural world, and arguably little of which is merely incidental. For great poetry this is often the norm. It is in trying to understand the significance of this imagery, I have found commentaries by those having researched the subject helpful, albeit not binding. Another rabbit hole, which I have resisted exploring over much is how the Song relates to contemporary love poetry regarding its possible use of sexual metaphors. Another challenge is working out who are the characters of the Song, assuming they are not merely made up, and piecing together what seems to be the story line. I give my view of who's who in the Song text included later.

While I recognise those who do identify two lovers: the king (Solomon) and the humble, rustic shepherd (both referred to in the Song), given Solomon's history with women was far removed from the biblical model of a man loving solely his one and only wife, having thought long and hard about it, I am inclined to the view the lover is Solomon, showing himself initially as that shepherd, possibly during one of his visits to one of his country estates, possibly incognito, and the beloved as a modest, Shulamite country girl, who despite his 999 other liaisons was to be his one true love. Some have speculated that Solomon wrote songs for all his wives. If so, this is his Song of songs. Then there is a third party, often referred to in the text as the "Daughters of Jerusalem" or by some commentators as "Friends" or as I prefer to call them – the "Chorus", who provide a helpful running commentary to what is going on.

The "Lover", the "Beloved" and the "Chorus", after the first verse, cover the entire rest of the Song as speaking parts, although other parties, such as the watchmen and the brothers, are referred to and play short cameo roles. The Song has been seen as a number of unrelated poems, although I am inclined to view it as a developing story starting with initial and testing love and ending with maturing and enduring love. But it may not be that simple, given the marriage may have been that in chapter 3, and we find that sexual intimacy is delicately alluded to in chapter 1 and sexual restraint in chapter 8. Some see the story darting backwards and forwards during this love affair, maybe helped by the inclusion of dreams. In arguing in favour of the developing love notion, we can see how an immature and tentative love alluded to in chapter 1 becomes a mature and confident one in chapter 8. Readers might adopt a view on all these matters, but it should not detract from what follows. Importantly, they are encouraged to study the Song for themselves and, while reaching a view there are some things we do not understand, are blessed by doing so.

It is not my intention to insist on any understanding I have reached, especially given my admission that while I know a lot more now than 50 years ago, when I first discovered the Song, but as they say: the more we know, the more we know we don't know. Given the wide discrepancy of views on interpretative frameworks by so many people better than me, these past 3000 years, without a key for doing so being available in Holy Scripture, puts the one we individually come up with in the "we can agree to disagree" category. Then there is the matter of getting to grips with the original language, made more challenging because the Song is poetry rather than prose, and coming to terms with the cultural context of which the rich imagery used is but a part.

The notion the Song is based on a real-life love story between king Solomon, initially disguised as a rustic shepherd, and an ordinary country lass, is therefore the one I have opted for. I hope it explains, partly at least, when it comes to daily meditations, why I have written as I have. I do so mindful, not only is there an important lesson to be derived concerning, as one learned friend put it, sexual ethics, but of a deep spiritual application for those intent on following the two great commands, about loving God with all that we have and loving our neighbour (that includes everyone) as ourselves. It is, on this basis, I offer these thoughts.

Finally, while it appears the Song is one of the few Bible books where prophecy does not feature, I argue – it does as it gives a foretaste of what it will be like when the Church sits down with Christ at the Marriage Supper of the Lamb. While I may be going out on a limb saying so, as we see the Beloved looking

Interpreting the Song

forward to her lover's return: "*Make haste, my beloved, and be thou like to a roe or to a young hart upon the mountains of spices*", it is something that should resonate with Christian believers as we look forward to Jesus' return.

Before moving on, I offer the following quotes, which have guided my thoughts:

"Heaven forbid any man in Israel ever disputed that the Song of Songs is holy. For the whole world is not worth the day on which the Song of Songs was given to Israel, for all the Writings are holy and the Song of Songs is holy of holies." **Rabbi Akiba (circa 100AD)**

"The Song of Solomon is regarded today as probably one of the most obscure and difficult books in the Bible. But it may surprise you to know that throughout the Christian centuries it has been one of the most read and most loved books of all. During the dark days before the Protestant Reformation when the Albaneses fled the Catholic church and John Huss led his small bands of Christians up into Bohemia, this was one of the books of the Bible that was frequently read, quoted, referred to and memorized. It was a great comfort to them. In the days after the Reformation, in the time of the bitter persecution of the Covenanters of Scotland, out of which came the Presbyterian Church under the leadership of John Knox and others, this again was one of the most frequently read and most often quoted books. It brought the Covenanters great comfort and sustained the spirits of those men and women who were hunted like animals throughout the mountains and glens of Europe." **Ray Steadman**

"In attempting to explore Solomon's masterpiece a little I feel quite guilty. I realise that I am but an amateur who is trespassing among the stars where only angels have right of way. The poem means so much to me that, great daring, I am venturing forward into it hoping that what has helped me so much may help someone else as well." **W.W.Vellacott**

"Because you're gorgeous I'd do anything for you. Because you're gorgeous I know you'll get me through." **Babybird**

"Can't buy me love, oh, Everybody tells me so, Can't buy me love, oh, No, no, no, no … I don't care too much for money, Money can't buy me love, Can't buy me love, oh Love, oh, Buy me love, oh." **The Beatles**

"For we are so preciously loved by God that we cannot even comprehend it. No created being can ever know how much and how sweetly and tenderly God loves them. It is only with the help of his grace that we are able to persevere in spiritual contemplation with endless won-

der at his high, surpassing, immeasurable love which our Lord in his goodness has for us." **Julian of Norwich**

"This Book has at all times been prized by the spiritually-minded. It is full of the heart's deep affections towards the Lord Jesus, and the utterance of love to Him is ever precious to those who are His." **John Jewell Penstone**

"Pope Benedict XVI's encyclical Deus Caritas Est (God is Love) of 2006 refers to the Song of Songs in both its literal and allegorical meaning, stating that erotic love (eros) and self donating love (agape) is shown there as the two halves of true love, which is both giving and receiving." **Wikipedia**

"As the bridegroom rejoiceth over the bride, so shall thy God rejoice over thee" **Isaiah 62:5**

"My heart is inditing a good matter: I speak of the things which I have made touching the king: my tongue is the pen of a ready writer." **Psalm 45:1**

> O Christ, He is the fountain,
> The deep, sweet well of life:
> Its living streams I've tasted
> Which save from grief and strife.
> And to an ocean fulness,
> His mercy doth expand;
> His grace is all-sufficient
> As by His wisdom planned.
>
> O I am my Beloved's,
> And my Beloved's mine;
> He brings a poor vile sinner
> Into His house of wine!
> I stand upon His merit;
> I know no other stand.
> I'm hidden in His presence
> And held by His own hand.
>
> The Bride eyes not her garment,
> But her dear Bridegroom's face;
> I will not gaze at glory,
> But on my King of grace:

Interpreting the Song

Not at the crown He giveth,
But on His pierced hand;
The Lamb is all the glory,
And my eternal stand!
Anne Ross Cousin (1824-1906)

It passeth knowledge, that dear love of Thine,
My Savior, Jesus; yet this soul of mine
Would of Thy love in all its breadth and length,
Its height and depth, its everlasting strength, Know more and more.

Oh, fill me, Jesus, Savior, with Thy love!
Lead, lead me to the living fount above;
Thither may I, in simple faith draw nigh,
And never to another fountain fly, But unto Thee.

Lord Jesus, when Thee face to face I see,
When on Thy lofty throne I sit with Thee,
Then of Thy love, in all its breadth and length,
Its height and depth, its everlasting strength, My soul shall sing.
Mary Shekleton (1827-1883)

Jesus, the very thought of Thee
With sweetness fills my breast;
But sweeter far Thy face to see,
And in Thy presence rest.
Nor voice can sing, nor heart can frame,
Nor can the memory find
A sweeter sound than Thy blest Name,
O Savior of mankind!

O Hope of every contrite heart,
O Joy of all the meek,
To those who fall, how kind Thou art!
How good to those who seek!
But what to those who find? Ah, this
Nor tongue nor pen can show;
The love of Jesus, what it is
None but His loved ones know.

O Jesus! light of all below!
Thou fount of life and fire!

Surpassing all the joys we know,
And all we can desire.
No other source have we but Thee,
Soul-thirst to satisfy.
Exhaustless spring! the waters free!
All other streams are dry.

Jesus, our only Joy be Thou,
As Thou our Prize wilt be;
Jesus, be Thou our Glory now,
And through eternity.
Bernard of Clairvaux (1090-1153)

Day 1: The Song of songs (1:1)

"The Song of songs, which is Solomon's."

Here we are introduced to this sublime song, this most sacred of books of the Bible. It is Solomon's song and it is his Song of songs. While Solomon was arguably the wisest man who ever lived, having been bestowed this gift by God himself, at Solomon's request so he could best rule God's own special people, as called upon by God to do, we also know he had 700 wives and 300 concubines, making it a point of wonderment that he was able to pronounce so profoundly and with such great understanding on what is meant as a unique, wonderful love relationship between a man and his one wife. The tragedy was he failed to apply those insights personally, a danger we all could face. Whether the Song was about what was his one true love or merely a commentary on how real love ought to be, we can't say for sure, but Solomon understood something incredibly important and was likely without peer in doing so. One of the challenges as we begin our journey of discovery of the riches contained in the Song is attaching a right understanding to the words that follow concerning Solomon's Song of songs.

Was it a reflection on the love between the divine and the human (Yahweh and Israel or Christ and His Church or even an individual believer) or was it about the love between Solomon or an unnamed rustic shepherd and this Shulamite girl or maybe a love triangle involving all these, we are meant to unravel? The thousands who have commentated on the Song in the 3000 years since the Song was penned do not agree on the matter (although a view is offered in the introductory chapters), but whatever the true interpretation is, it should not be a barrier to finding spiritual edification or practical application given it is scripture and we are reminded *"All scripture is given by inspiration of God, and is for doctrine, for reproof, for correction, for instruction in righteousness:"* (2 Timothy 3:16). As for it being the Song of songs, we know it is one of 1005 that Solomon wrote. It is the only one we are fully aware of and the one the Holy Spirit has allowed to be included fully in holy canon, even though many down the ages have questioned its right to be there. It should be remembered this is poetry rather that prose and is to be sung rather than read; and as such it is meant to speak to the heart more than the mind; that it should engage all senses, even if only in our imagination, and deal with all ranges of human emotions, especially love.

Like Rabbi Akiba, one may view delving into this song as akin to entering the Holy of holies. It should be done reverently just as did the High Priest in ancient Israel when he entered there, into the presence of an awesome God, the Holy One of Israel. Let it be so when it comes to our meditating on *the Song of songs, which is Solomon's.*

Day 2: Intimate love (1:2)

"Let him kiss me with the kisses of his mouth: for thy love is better than wine."

The first thing that might strike us as we get started on the Song proper is that it wastes no time when it comes to what the Song is about and also leaves us in little doubt that, even though it was written by a man, it seeks to present the girl's own perspective, although some may say in a chauvinistic way, which is one desiring pure intimacy. While the man does get to speak, the girl appears to dominate the conversation, even if by virtue of ending up saying twice as much as the man.

At the start, we find she wants to be kissed and not just a chaste peck that a brother may give to his sister but the passionate kisses of a lover. If one were to use a word to encapsulate the essence of the Song, it would be intimacy, not in a crude or lustful way, but rather in a way that is pure and innocent. The girl craves the love of her lover, more than anything else, begging the question regarding those we love, whether our earthly spouse or our heavenly lover, concerning which – how and to what extent do we yearn for His presence and seek and desire to do what pleases Him ahead of any other consideration? A kiss, if nothing else, symbolises and is a token of that love. In comparing love, she does so with wine, begging the question why wine? We may enjoy wine and welcome drinking in moderation. If nothing else, it can add to enjoyment when eating a meal and helps to release inhibitions and add to bonhomie. As good as wine is, the Lover's love is far better. The challenge of the verses that are to follow is how we go about developing and maintaining that love.

Regarding the next two verses, firstly by the Beloved: *"Because of the savour of thy good ointments thy name is as ointment poured forth, therefore do the virgins love thee. Draw me, we will run after thee: the king hath brought me into his chambers"* to which the Chorus who are so impressed wished to join in: *"we will be glad and rejoice in thee, we will remember thy love more than wine: the upright love thee"*, and we are now introduced to some of the outstanding qualities of the Lover, that does the drawing. These include his good name, which is *compared to ointment* poured forth. It was his good name that attracted people to him, whether the virgins or the upright, which reminds us of the importance of having a good name, no better revealed than in the person of Jesus, and of avoiding doing that which may tarnish that good name. But as far as this song is concerned, the girl wants to be drawn and the lover (here revealed as the king) is able to grant her what she wished, with gladness and rejoicing being the result, not forgetting that his love that is better than wine is something exceedingly worth having.

Day 3: Black and comely (1:5)

"I am black, but comely, O ye daughters of Jerusalem, as the tents of Kedar, as the curtains of Solomon."

As far as true love is concerned, it is, or should be, blind when it comes to colour, and the language used here is not racist. As far as the culture the girl related to goes (unlike my own western culture) fairness was associated with beauty, and she was *not* fair. For in the next verse, she explains: *"Look not upon me, because I am black, because the sun hath looked upon me: my mother's children were angry with me; they made me the keeper of the vineyards; but mine own vineyard have I not kept"*. We now know the reason; she had been working in the sun on vineyards not her own, as directed by her brothers, who were angry with her. A consequence of this activity, besides losing her fairness by being exposed to the sun, was that she neglected her own vineyard, which maybe is something we should be mindful of when we go around doing what is not our principal responsibility and ignoring that which is. The vineyard, like the garden we come across later, is virtually synonymous with the girl herself, but it is her responsibility and should be her priority, to look after it.

Her blackness is compared with the *"tents of Kedar"* and the *"curtains of Solomon"* and is our introduction to the Song's figurative language, in which it abounds. Notwithstanding her fixation on her blackness, she is still aware she is comely and addresses her remarks to the daughters of Jerusalem, which like the rich imagery is to be a recurring theme of the Song. Perhaps, we too can take comfort that, despite our flaws, our own lover might still be attracted to us anyway. Not to be satisfied with being a mere spectator, like members of the Chorus she addresses, she embarks on her quest to seek out the Lover, asking directions: *"Tell me, O thou whom my soul loveth, where thou feedest, where thou makest thy flock to rest at noon: for why should I be as one that turneth aside by the flocks of thy companions? If thou know not, O thou fairest among women, go thy way forth by the footsteps of the flock, and feed thy kids beside the shepherds' tents"* (1:7,8). This may be a good example for us to follow!

The Chorus can also see beauty in the girl and are happy to direct her. We might take encouragement that, despite negative aspects in our journey and a realisation we may not be all we ought, there may still be positives and, even if we may not see them, others may. While being "black" for whatever reason could be seen negatively, we may be seen as "comely" by the one who matters most and rather than stay put, we should seek out our heavenly lover so we can be with him.

Day 4: Horses and chariots (1:9)

"I have compared thee, O my love, to a company of horses in Pharaoh's chariots."

Having succeeded in her quest to be united with her lover, he makes an unusual observation, to which he elaborates "*Thy cheeks are comely with rows of jewels, thy neck with chains of gold*" (1:10) and proposes an unusual refinement "*We will make thee borders of gold with studs of silver*" (1:11). We brace ourselves for the future with the sort of imagery which abounds in this Song, and are introduced to the notion that what is already there, however basic, can be enhanced.

As far as this meditation goes, like with much of the figurative language used in the Song, our understanding may be incomplete and, in trying to understand, we may ask why this metaphor of horses (mares were referred to here, rather than stallions which we might normally expect to be used), as well as Pharoah's chariots was used. It is one of many questions we might ask Solomon if we ever get to meet him. One imagines that Solomon, when contemplating his possessions, took special pride in his horses.

As for interpretation … being harnessed to Pharaoh's chariots required a special type of horse and no doubt with the finery used they made a splendid sight. The indications are that horses from Egypt were the best and this was the reason they were imported into Israel. There would have been a sense of wildness about the horses and the qualities seen here were part of their natural beauty. We can only imagine Solomon being besotted by this untamed beauty, so full of mystery and potential, which can be harnessed and built upon, just like these Egyptian imports.

There was also a further sense of ever readiness as their task was not just for ceremonial purposes but to take the king and his armies into battle, and in order to do so the horses needed to be strong and swift. By making the comparisons he does, Solomon bestows on the girl the highest of honours and the greatest of confidences. In adding to the qualities already there, "*borders of gold*" and "*studs of silver*", the horses become even more magnificent to behold, but these were not merely for show but were a practical addition in the service of the king.

We might reflect that as we come to our heavenly lover with whatever natural attributes we possess, we are far from the finished product and we are very much work in progress, but he is happy to work with us and in us. We should not dismiss our natural attributes yet we may always recognise that He can rightly take what we have, add to it whatever is missing and gladly use us in His royal service.

Day 5: Thou art fair (1:15)

"Behold, thou art fair, my love; behold, thou art fair; thou hast doves' eyes."

We learn here of the lover's appreciation and admiration for the girl, a point that is to be repeated several times in the Song. One of the observations of life we may make is the number of people that have low self-esteem, and significantly as far as some of our experiences goes this is true amongst many earnest Christians, but more important than that is not how we see ourselves but how God sees us. A key gospel theme to recall is *"He brings a poor vile sinner into His house of wine"*.

Whether or not we see this as a description made from a human or divine perspective, the point should be made that as far as the lover is concerned, the beloved is fair and is loved regardless of how she feels about herself or how others might see her – a principle seen throughout the Bible. Not that he needed to do so, but he repeats *thou art fair*. The main attribute of the girl cited here is her *doves' eyes*. When we think of a dove, we see something pure, gentle and innocent and as for the eyes of the dove these are single and there is no hint of crookedness in them. It is quite likely the girl in question really is that innocent and the danger for all of us as we experience the harsh realities and hard knocks of life is we can lose that innocence and become hard and devious. We need to *be wise as serpents* but at the same time need to be *harmless as doves*.

But it would be unsound exegesis to ignore the context for this verse and, even though innocence has been portrayed, it is part of a scene that included physical love making, leaving little to the imagination. Prior to his declaration of admiration the girl declares: *"A bundle of myrrh is my well beloved unto me; he shall lie all night betwixt my breasts. My beloved is unto me as a cluster of camphire in the vineyards of Engedi"* (1:13,14). After it is the lover's turn: *"Behold, thou art fair, my beloved, yea, pleasant: also our bed is green. The beams of our house are cedar, and our rafters of fir"* (1:16,17).

Taken alone, and within the human and divine context, this verse reassures us that the one we love sees us as fair despite our propensity for screwing things up and when it dawns on us what despicable people we can be. But like so much of the Song, we are encouraged to hang in there because of the one who remains faithful. But we cannot ignore the application when it comes to the physical love that was imagined. In a world where sex is often depicted in sordid terms, it is well to remember that God got in first and when the relationship is as it should be, and within the context of a faithful marriage relationship, sex is a very good thing.

Day 6: The Rose of Sharon (2:1)

"I am the rose of Sharon, and the lily of the valleys."

The first thing that might come to mind when we come across phrases like *rose of Sharon* and *lily of the valleys* is these are about things that are exotic and perhaps rare. One understanding, however, is that these plants, while presenting a pleasing picture to the eye, are common place in the land where this Song is set and if one were walking by might be trod upon without further thought, or like the pretty flowers on the tangle weed in my garden, pulled up and thrown out.

The girl didn't regard herself as special, as she likens herself to something quite common place, making it all the more remarkable from her perspective that her lover saw in her something special. While it is not healthy to put oneself down, which in the early days of this relationship she tended to do, it is not good either to have an inflated opinion of one's merits and remaining humble is a good thing. It is one quality that will have attracted her lover, when as far as the girl was concerned he could choose from any number of creditable candidates.

One cause of wonderment is that Christ chooses us when there are so many other beautiful flowers that he might choose from. The matter of free will and election has long divided the church, but here we see both the girl seek out her lover and he her. Incidentally, this is one of many examples in the Song where the man seems to be portrayed as someone superior compared with the woman, one reason to think this is about more than a human only relationship. A man woman relationship should be seen as between two equals, both with a mixture of good and bad points that in order to develop needs to be accommodated.

The lover's instant response to the girl's self-deprecation is "*as the lily among thorns, so is my love among the daughters*" (2.2), indicating whatever she thought about herself his view on her outstanding features was so much higher than her own and being among thorns makes her stand out even more. It is a sobering thought that amidst all the niceties the world around the girl was full of thorns. She was in his eyes the stand out "*lily among thorns*", putting her so much above the rest and thereby was to be afforded a special place of honour.

Within human love, it is well to take the view that the lucky one that one's lover has set his/her desire on is me. Even more so in the divine human love relationship to think that someone who is a mere *lily of the valley* should have been *chosen beforehand in him from before the foundation of the universe* (Ephesians 1:4).

Day 7: The Apple Tree (2:3)

"As the apple tree among the trees of the wood, so is my beloved among the sons. I sat down under his shadow with great delight, and his fruit was sweet to my taste."

The exchange begun in 2:1 continues. Just as he describes his beloved as *the lily among thorns* so she describes her lover as *the apple tree among the trees of the wood*. In both cases, each one describes the other as outstanding among his/her peers. There will be speculation as to what sort of tree this was but a number of things are clear besides being one to stand out when compared with the other trees in the wood. It gave shade to them by virtue of its foliage, which is for all the year round for those who sat under it, and as for its fruit it was sweet and satisfying.

In a husband/wife relationship, the traditional role of the man is to be a protector of and provider for his wife, while the wife is meant to support her husband. Such assigning of roles may well be downplayed in our modern culture that lauds equality and discourages manly men, but it is biblical. Rather than merely bowing to pressure by going along with today's cultural norms, the husband should remember his responsibility to protect and provide for his wife. When looking at the comparison relationship of God or Christ with Israel or the Church, we find a similar principle applies. We have a divine protector but we need to respond in love. Outside of that relationship, there can be no guarantee of protection and provision, even though there could be and often is the false allure of something that might appear better, which doesn't require the same constancy and commitment. But the assurance given here is that, regardless of the turmoil and conflict we may find raging all around us, we can sit under this particular apple tree and find refuge and cover from the elements and whatever it is the world may choose to throw at us. We can also apply this to how it could be in marriage.

There may be many things we might do well to take note of, as we look around at what might disturb us, but we are able to find delight under His shadow regardless. There may be fruit to be found elsewhere that appears desirable and sweet to taste but it may also leave a bitter taste. The fruit our heavenly lover provides is sweet inasmuch it not only tastes good and pleasant but that it sustains and satisfies us fully. If there is any encouragement, it is simply to sit under this particular apple tree and not to go in search of another; for this is where we need to be.

The delights that can be found in our Lord and heavenly lover will far exceed anything the world can offer. And as we will see later, this lover stands head and shoulders above any other like *the apple tree among the trees of the wood*.

Day 8: His banner over me (2:4)

"He brought me to the banqueting house, and his banner over me was love."

One of the impacts this Song has had down the centuries is it has helped to inspire successive generations of song writers, *e.g.* "*Jesus, our only joy be Thou, As Thou our prize wilt be; Jesus, be Thou our glory now, And through eternity*". We might remember a popular song based on this very verse (along with the actions): "*He brought me to His banqueting table; His banner over me is love*".

Banners invariably are associated with a message that the banner provider or waver wishes to show to any who look upon it. We are at the point when the king is wanting to show off his bride (new?) to his entourage/watching crowd. As for the banqueting house, this is a place for sumptuous feasting in a convivial setting and the person in this case that is to be honoured is the bride. As for the beloved, she has come a long way from being that humble shepherdess, a non-entity as far as the world goes, and is now in this exalted position where her lover is desirous and able to display his affection to her before all onlookers without any thought of recrimination. Think, what a happy position to be in! Banners can and do display all sorts of messages and it is something invariably waved before a watching world to make a point. There is little doubt in this case what that message is, summed up in a single word – *love*. The bridegroom is letting everyone know that this is the person he loves and wishes to spend the rest of his life with. There is little doubt that whatever the time or prevailing beliefs that love is the one that most will identify with as being there toward the top.

Much has been written (and sung) about love, perhaps more than any other subject (and is the one thing that bemuses and occupies human thinking above any), and few would dispute that it is a most wonderful thing even though unrequited, betrayed and perverted love are some of the sad digressions we may encounter when it comes to love. When it comes to love and banquets, one glorious prospect for Christ lovers is the enticing prospect of joining him at the marriage supper of the Lamb. For those invited to the supper the banner over them will be love.

Going back to the aforementioned action song – those being brought to His banqueting house were those singing the song and the bringer was Christ Himself. We have no right to expect such a wonderful reception, being all too aware of our flaws and shortcomings, and we can only do so because of His grace. The message to the world we can take on board is that He has afforded us this undeserved and unexpected honour and He is not ashamed to declare to all that He loves us.

Day 9: Not to stir up love (2:7)

"I charge you, O ye daughters of Jerusalem, by the roes, and by the hinds of the field, that ye stir not up, nor awake my love, till he please."

Following the girl being brought into her lover's banqueting house (2:4), we can now see her yearning for his love and longing for his embrace: *"Stay me with flagons, comfort me with apples: for I am sick of love. His left hand is under my head, and his right hand doth embrace me"* (2:5,6) and it is at this point she charges the daughters of Jerusalem with a call that is later to be repeated: *"I charge you, O ye daughters of Jerusalem, by the roes, and by the hinds of the field, that ye stir not up, nor awake my love, till he please"* (3:5) and then again, but this time without invoking roes and hinds: *"I charge you, O daughters of Jerusalem, that ye stir not up, nor awake my love, until he please."* (8:4)

We can speculate who the daughters of Jerusalem are but we do know they take an active interest in all that is going on, and were close to the king, albeit not enjoying the same intimacy that the girl enjoyed, being both a "daughter" and belonging to the place where the king had his throne. We might surmise as to the significance of hinds and roes, starting with their association with the natural world and implication they were chosen as representative of youthful vigour. Why she implores, not once but three times, the daughters of Jerusalem not to *awake my love, until he please* could be in part down to sometimes patience being needed. It is well to wait sometimes and recognise the Lord acts in His own time.

True love cannot be whipped up by noise, emotion or anything else come to that, but when it comes to this relationship it can only happen when he deigns it is to happen (and thank God, He is the instigator). The love that is depicted in this Song is more real than anything that might be manufactured by human intervention. It is something authentic and to be experienced, and not merely something that she or others talk about. Just maybe in the everyday happenings of life, things need to just simply happen and the couple must do what needs doing based on that love.

As for us and our heavenly lover, the thrice repeating of this injunction at various stages in this relationship indicates firstly that love is always there and is the basis of all that later transpires and is not something that can be contrived according to whim. The truth is that He will rest in His love for *"The Lord thy God in the midst of thee is mighty; he will save, he will rejoice over thee with joy; he will rest in his love, he will joy over thee with singing"* (Zephaniah 3:17).

Day 10: Leaping upon the mountains (2:8)

"The voice of my beloved! behold, he cometh leaping upon the mountains, skipping upon the hills."

One of the abiding images of this song is of the youthful vigour, the abundance of energy and the ability to do what the lover desires, even if humanly speaking it is only barely possible, irrespective of whatever obstacles and challenges there are on the way, on the lover's part. This picture is further reinforced in the next verse when he reveals himself, to begin with in part only, to his beloved: *"My beloved is like a roe or a young hart: behold, he standeth behind our wall, he looketh forth at the windows, shewing himself through the lattice"* (2:9). This joyful exuberance is later repeated: *"Until the day break, and the shadows flee away, turn, my beloved, and be thou like a roe or a young hart upon the mountains of Bether"* (2:17) as the girl further delights in this realisation and takes comfort from her lover's interest in her and encourages him to continue to be like the roe or the hart, hopeful and confident that she and he will soon be together, and he will overcome all obstacles that might appear to prevent this.

It is worth reflecting first on the lover's voice. It was distinctive and delightful to her ear. For those who follow Christ, this should also resonate like that of sheep led by the Good Shepherd; we hear his voice and follow him. Surely it is his voice in which we delight and it is to his call we should respond. Much of that which attracts him to us is to do with his flawless character that no human lover can ever possess, and which is a major pre-occupation of this Song. But to begin, he is *"leaping upon the mountains"* and *"skipping upon the hills"*, as if without a care in the world and, what might be seen as obstacles (mountains and hills), present no barrier at all and are readily negotiated because he is able to do so.

For those of us who are old, the thought of leaping upon mountains and skipping upon hills is not a realistic prospect compared with what we might have attempted in our youth, but the intent of doing so in order to reach out toward our beloved should not go away, only our limits to deliver. But not so with Christ our lover, who is ever willing and able to skip on hills and leap on mountains, promising to his disciples *"I am with you always, even unto the end of the world"* (Matthew 28:20) and with whom we might say *"I can do all things through Christ which strengtheneth me"* (Philippians 4:13), for it is he who can do it through us and does. While we may be daunted by this formidable array of obstacles, we need to take heart and be confident that this is a small thing for our heavenly lover.

Day 11: My fair one come away (2:10)

"My beloved spake, and said unto me, Rise up, my love, my fair one, and come away."

The lover, who we have just found out in the verse before was he who: "*standeth behind our wall, he looketh forth at the windows, shewing himself through the lattice*", is now telling the girl "*rise up, my love, my fair one, and come away*" with him. He gives the reason "*lo, the winter is past, the rain is over and gone; The flowers appear on the earth; the time of the singing of birds is come, and the voice of the turtle is heard in our land; The fig tree putteth forth her green figs, and the vines with the tender grape give a good smell*" (11-13) before repeating his request: "*arise, my love, my fair one, and come away*".

It would have been easy to stay put, in her comfort zone, surrounded by all that was familiar, but it was now time to venture forth, into uncharted territory with her lover to lead and guide her. For one thing, the winter had passed. The cold and lack of growth and lack of life in the natural world was no longer. What was before her, should she respond, were the joys of Spring: birds singing, including the sound of the turtle dove, fig trees putting forth figs and vines producing tender grapes. She is ever his love, his fair one, but the choice was hers to stay put or venture forth. She is his "*dove, that art in the clefts of the rock, in the secret places of the stairs*" (2:14) but not to remain hidden. He asks to "*see her countenance … hear her voice*", "*for sweet is thy voice, and thy countenance is comely*".

Just as the girl was offered the choice to stay or go (to miss or find blessing) so we who sincerely seek to follow Christ are offered a similar choice. We could so easily hold back, as sadly many do, and thus lose out on so many of the blessings he wishes to shower on us and opportunities for us to be a blessing to other people. If we do venture out, we will be entering the unknown, may be misunderstood, suffer hardship and in any case will need to trust on Christ to lead us. Put like this, the choice is an obvious one (and, as we will see, the girl was to make the right choice) but for those of us who love Christ we too need to make that choice. While God in His grace can and does make up for our wrong decisions, like not taking up the opportunities that present themselves, it is sad that for some/many that is what they do decide and with it the thought of what might have been if they had ventured forth. Right now, Christ calls his loved ones: "*rise up, my love, my fair one, and come away*" and the answer to the question must be responded to on an individual basis – do I or don't I? Deep down, we know the right response!

Day 12: Taking the little foxes (2:15)

"Take us the foxes, the little foxes, that spoil the vines: for our vines have tender grapes."

One of the first challenges facing the girl, who has just taken up her lover's gracious offer: *rise up, my love, my fair one, and come away* (2:10,14) is to look after the vineyards that we see as belonging not to "her" or "him" but to both. Vineyards, as we see elsewhere in the Song, are a recurring theme. It can be taken to represent the girl as a person or that which she has responsibility for. The purpose behind any vineyard is to produce grapes to make wine. But if grapes are not looked after, they won't survive and the vine will produce little, poor or no fruit, especially as at this *tender* phase they need special care and attention.

That which can spoil the vines are little foxes, that which might go unnoticed if not observant or careful. Before you know it, if unchecked they can cause havoc. We might well ask what exactly this creature or figure of speech stands for but whatever it is, it is something significant. It appears the girl had been negligent in her duties. It is quite clear to any offering guidance to married couples that for that relationship to remain strong and healthy, and not end up in breakdown, as many do, it needs to be worked on, and not just by the woman! Here we may feel irritation at Solomon if that was how he felt – catching foxes was his job too after all! The bottom line is to identify what might ruin that relationship and deal with it. The obvious parallel is between me and Christ, where the duty of working on the vineyard is down to me, albeit with his support. There are all sorts of things that can get in the way, and often do and spoil what is meant to be good.

We can think of all sorts of examples of bad attitudes, thoughts, habits, actions etc., where the antidote is the fruit of the Spirit: *love, joy, peace, longsuffering, gentleness, goodness, faith, meekness, temperance* (Galatians 5:22,23). Pertinent are Jesus' words: *"I am the true vine, and my Father is the husbandman. Every branch in me that beareth not fruit he taketh away: and every branch that beareth fruit, he purgeth it, that it may bring forth more fruit"* (John 15:1,2), indicating that bearing fruit, as indeed we must, can be a painful process – thus the pruning.

These may be, on the face of it, tiny sins but as these continue to mount, and are not dealt with, we will find that we don't enjoy the wonderful relationship that we ought to, and so it wanes and sometimes appears to be lost forever. The solution is to follow the lover's counsel: *"take us the foxes, the little foxes, that spoil the vines"* realising we are doing it both for him and me. And it is best to do so early while the tender grapes are on the vine, so these are not lost forever.

Day 13: My beloved is mine (2:16)

"My beloved is mine, and I am his: he feedeth among the lilies."

We come to perhaps the most powerful depiction of the love between the two lovers, when the girl declares: *"my beloved is mine, and I am his"*. There is little doubt this love was enduring and constant, and it was fully reciprocated. The call was to be repeated *"I am my beloved's, and my beloved is mine: he feedeth among the lilies."* (6:3) and again *"I am my beloved's, and his desire is toward me"* (7:10). The second time the order is reversed – her belonging to him comes first, and third time round her ownership doesn't even feature for it is all about him, which one commentator saw as evidence of what was a maturing love. But for now she is content to lay claim on her lover – he is mine, as if to say there is nothing anyone can do about it, for the matter is settled, just as was the case with the converse *"I am his"*. We are soon to see this love being tested and that which will see the lovers through such a time is the love they have for one another, irrespective of the trials.

For Christians, theirs is not so much a matter of religious adherence but rather that of a relationship between the believer and his/her Lord and Saviour but as far as the *"my beloved is mine and I am his"* claim is concerned we might well add "Lover". Paul's prayer is apt: *"that Christ may dwell in your hearts by faith; that ye, being rooted and grounded in love, may be able to comprehend with all saints what is the breadth, and length, and depth, and height; and to know the love of Christ, which passeth knowledge, that ye might be filled with all the fulness of God."* (Ephesians 3:17-19). While the harder realities of everyday life might bring out thoughts more down to earth, we do well to ponder our relationship as one that applies to each waking moment and then into eternity. This is what will comfort and sustain us in the testing days and hard knocks of life ahead of us.

But she doesn't stop there, for she declares *he feedeth among the lilies*. As was pointed out earlier, those who emphasise the spiritual and a more allegorical meaning to the Song may interpret this differently to those who emphasise the literal and a more human meaning. We leave it for readers to decide whether this is more to do with his having fellowship with God's people or to do with physical love making (one might take a view that it can be with both), but importantly the image conveyed here is of a lover who is content. The love described by the girl is not merely for her benefit but his also, and it brings us to a key element of love – it is to do with both giving and receiving. The two lovers give to each other.

Day 14: Lost and found (3:1)

"By night on my bed I sought him whom my soul loveth: I sought him, but I found him not."

We have here the first of two "lost and found" mini adventures involving the two lovers, and recounted from the girl's perspective. It is possible, in this case the girl was merely dreaming of her lover and him not being with her. Why she should think so we can't say for sure, but it is not uncommon for this to happen (we all succumb to doubts) despite the undisputed fact as far as she was concerned: *I am his and he is mine.* Doubts can creep in so subtly and quickly, made more likely by her being alone at night laid on her bed. This can be distressing, especially if the expectation is for her lover's continuous presence.

Her response was quick and decisive: "*I will rise now, and go about the city in the streets, and in the broad ways I will seek him whom my soul loveth*" (3:2) but it was to no avail: "*I sought him, but I found him not.*", adding to her feelings of anxiety. Then she tries a different approach or rather avails herself of an opportunity that presents itself: "*The watchmen that go about the city found me: to whom I said, Saw ye him whom my soul loveth?*" (3:3) Who these watchmen are we can't say for sure, but it seems their role was to look after the safety of those living in the city. Soon after we find: "*It was but a little that I passed from them, but I found him whom my soul loveth:*" She is so happy with her find: "*I held him, and would not let him go, until I had brought him into my mother's house, and into the chamber of her that conceived me*" (3:3,4).

As young Christians, we are sometimes told not to rely on feelings but on faith, holding onto the promise of *him whom my soul loveth* that he will never desert us. To bring in the "*soul*" is likely to emphasise that she loved him from deep within. There may be times when our heavenly lover seems far from us but it is not he that has gone away. In the second lost and found incident described in chapter 5 the problem was likely to do with wilful sin that had crept into her life, but on this occasion, it was likely more to do with her placing feelings above that of faith.

Like the girl, we will be tested, and we will feel (and be) isolated; for it is almost guaranteed, but like her who cherished the relationship she enjoys with her lover so highly, we do well to take whatever measures are needed to ensure that relationship is secure and recognise we live by faith, and not by sight. One of the beautiful pictures of saints of the past is they enjoyed an ever-present sense of closeness (intimacy) with the Lord they loved, from mundane to marvellous.

Day 15: The King in his splendour (3:6)

"Who is this that cometh out of the wilderness like pillars of smoke, perfumed with myrrh and frankincense, with all powders of the merchant?"

We come to a strange scene in our story of love between two lovers. Solomon is named, who we can take to be the lover (although some see it differently). Up to now the girl may have only known Solomon in the guise of a shepherd and his promise he will return to take her as his bride. Whether she had realised up to that point that he was indeed the king, we can't say for sure, and that being the case this would have come as a surprise and any pretence there might have been on Solomon's part now goes. He comes with his entourage from out of the wilderness, perfumed with myrrh and frankincense, two gifts the Magi gave the baby Jesus and just as sobering, this was also linked to him in his death and burial. The girl asks *"who is this"*, maybe not yet convinced it was her lover that had returned for her. Later, a related question is asked about the girl: *"who is this that cometh up from the wilderness"* (8:5), and we sense the procession was complete.

It is an impressive sight: *"Behold his bed, which is Solomon's; threescore valiant men are about it, of the valiant of Israel. They all hold swords, being expert in war: every man hath his sword upon his thigh because of fear in the night. King Solomon made himself a chariot of the wood of Lebanon. He made the pillars thereof of silver, the bottom thereof of gold, the covering of it of purple, the midst thereof being paved with love, for the daughters of Jerusalem* (3:7-10). We can't profess to understand all the symbolism or why special attention to the daughters of Jerusalem (Zion) but she invites them to behold the king (her lover) for she is so delighted with him (as we should be with ours) *"Go forth, O ye daughters of Zion, and behold king Solomon with the crown wherewith his mother crowned him in the day of his espousals, and in the day of the gladness of his heart"* (3:11).

As to how we connect this episode into this story of love, one suggestion is that this is the point in the story when marriage actually takes place, as indeed it must happen, as this is the proper setting for the sexual intimacy, more than alluded to in the Song. For those who love Christ, even though we have not seen Him, we look forward to the time when He will come for His Bride (the Church) and we will not merely behold Him in His kingly splendour but we will be wedded to Him for evermore. This is He who was despised and rejected by men, suffered a cruel death on Calvary's cross and who will soon return to reign on the earth: King of kings and Lord of lords.

Day 16: Like a flock of goats (4:1)

"Behold, thou art fair, my love; behold, thou art fair; thou hast doves' eyes within thy locks: thy hair is as a flock of goats, that appear from mount Gilead."

Thus begins one of a number of descriptions of the girl given by her lover. It continues: *"Thy teeth are like a flock of sheep that are even shorn, which came up from the washing; whereof every one bear twins, and none is barren among them. Thy lips are like a thread of scarlet, and thy speech is comely: thy temples are like a piece of a pomegranate within thy locks. Thy neck is like the tower of David builded for an armoury, whereon there hang a thousand bucklers, all shields of mighty men. Thy two breasts are like two young roes that are twins, which feed among the lilies"* (4:2-5). Descriptions that follow along similar lines are found 6:4-9 and 7:1-6. We choose not to comment on this further description here, despite it being both challenging and profitable. That the lover is employing figurative language, using imagery his beloved was familiar with, there is little doubt, begging the question if it were a painting what it would look like.

Back to our meditation, a similar verse is found: *"Turn away thine eyes from me, for they have overcome me: thy hair is as a flock of goats that appear from Gilead"* (6:5). That she is fair as far as he is concerned we have little doubt, repeating what he said (1:15) and drawing attention again to her *dove's eyes* and pointing out her locks that part hide the eyes and is suggesting a degree of modesty and understated wisdom. There is something special about her eyes that he finds disturbing, for he asks her to turn them away as they have overcome him. But from both 4:1 and 6:5 we find he does draw attention to her hair, something ladies often pay special attention to, which is described *"as a flock of goats that appear from mount Gilead"*. Why hair; why goats and why Gilead are three questions that might stump us, but that is ok, because we don't have to come up with all the answers or be put off by our failure to do so. Many learned folk have tried and got it wrong, as they have with the interpretation of other body parts.

If I were to attempt to read Solomon's mind on the matter, I can imagine he would be familiar with Gilead (mentioned a number of times in scripture) and no doubt flocks of goats could be found grazing in its grasslands. Hair was a source of strength, e.g. Samson (Judges 16) and the Nazarites. It was linked to obedience. It may indicate submission in the case of women, seen as part of her beauty. For as strange as it may seem, his beloved's hair and a flock of goats appearing from mount Gilead are connected and form part of her beauty that so attracts her to him.

Day 17: A heart that is ravished (4:9)

"Thou hast ravished my heart, my sister, my spouse; thou hast ravished my heart with one of thine eyes, with one chain of thy neck."

This verse comes in the middle of a speech by the lover heaping praises on his beloved. He repeats *"thou art all fair my love"* (4:7) and makes the remarkable claim *"there is no spot in thee"*, given on her own admission and, as evidenced in earlier chapters, there are defects in character as well as appearance. Something amazing about God is He can see us both as rotten and spotless. The lover sees only perfection, which in a way should not surprise us as lovers are often blind to faults in their loved ones especially early on in a relationship before adjusting to each other's faults. He repeats his earlier plea (2:10) to come away, inviting her to see the world with him and from a higher place: *"come with me from Lebanon, my spouse, with me from Lebanon: look from the top of Amana, from the top of Shenir and Hermon, from the lions' dens, from the mountains of the leopards"*.

He proceeds to make further pronouncements *"Thou hast ravished my heart, my sister, my spouse; thou hast ravished my heart with one of thine eyes, with one chain of thy neck. How fair is thy love, my sister, my spouse! how much better is thy love than wine! and the smell of thine ointments than all spices! Thy lips, O my spouse, drop as the honeycomb: honey and milk are under thy tongue; and the smell of thy garments is like the smell of Lebanon."* (4:9-11). Ravish is a strong yet apt description of the effect one look of one of her eyes has had on him and the appearance of her stately neck, which just prior was described as a tower, where the shields of a thousand mighty men were hung from (4:4).

In applying this to the relationship we might have with our own heavenly lover, we can reflect once again, irrespective of how we might think of ourselves, he sees those who respond to his love as fair and by virtue of his atoning blood and our response to him there is no spot to be found. One of the great imponderables of life is why the Almighty and Holy God should create humankind knowing full well we would rebel and then in order to redeem us in the only way that was possible He sent His only Son (our heavenly lover) to be our atoning sacrifice and heavenly husband, and here we have granted a glimpse into this mystery.

Having been so ravished, He proceeds to take delight in those who respond to His call and will lead us out to accomplish his grand purposes in His creation. This is not something to be taken lightly but is a truth to be humbly received in awe, to think God's beloved Son might choose to take pleasure in His Bride, the Church.

Day 18: A garden inclosed (4:12)

"A garden inclosed is my sister, my spouse; a spring shut up, a fountain sealed."

Having been earlier introduced to the motif of a vineyard, we now have that of a garden. In both cases these relate to, and in this case is synonymous with, the girl herself. We note it is a walled garden that can only be entered into by the lover, who holds the keys, and is both her husband and her brother (a term that was to be repeated (5:1,2)). Given the imagery that is then presented is that of a sensuous nature and could be taken as to do with the act of making love, it is well to remember that such activity, at least as far as God is concerned, is exclusive, only for those who are married to each other. Within the garden is a *spring shut up* and *a fountain sealed*, serving the garden alone, without which the fruits and spices we are about to be introduced to would not be able to flourish.

Regarding which, as far as the garden goes, *"thy plants are an orchard of pomegranates, with pleasant fruits; camphire, with spikenard. Spikenard and saffron; calamus and cinnamon, with all trees of frankincense; myrrh and aloes, with all the chief spices"* (4:13,14) and, once again, we are brought back to the importance of water, whether to do specifically with making love or reminiscent of the life giving water that comes from heaven itself, like that which Jesus promised to those who believe on him *"he that believeth on me, as the scripture hath said, out of his belly shall flow rivers of living water. This spake he of the Spirit, which they that believe on him should receive"* (John 7:38,39). Here the water is presented as *"a fountain of gardens, a well of living waters, and streams from Lebanon* (4:15). As far as the lover is concerned, his beloved is that garden yielding a wonderful array of fruits and spices that he looks forward to enjoying.

As we reflect upon our own relationship with our own heavenly lover, it is well to realise that the whole of our life is that garden, the purpose of which it to yield all manner of delights for the one we love. But, in order to do so, it needs watering, given the rivers of living waters promised by Jesus to His disciples is also the activity of the Holy Spirit and is the work of the Holy Spirit that enables us to be fruitful. Gardens also need to be cultivated or else they will be overcome with weeds etc. As we consider our duties and priorities, which can be many and various, the overriding consideration should surely be that of yielding fruit that is pleasing to Him and for our lives to be a sweet-smelling savour so he can delight in its aroma and involves us in lovingly tending our (his) garden. When tempted to stray, we should remember who the garden is meant for (human and divine).

Day 19: North and south winds (4:16)

"Awake, O north wind; and come, thou south; blow upon my garden, that the spices thereof may flow out. Let my beloved come into his garden, and eat his pleasant fruits."

We have seen that for any garden to flourish it needs to be watered and cultivated. Yet there are certain things, humanly speaking, that can't be controlled but if present might add to the delights that are on offer. We talk now about the wind, specifically the north wind and the south wind, without which it will not be possible to enjoy the sweet smells that result from these blowing in the garden.

North and south winds are quite different when it comes to intensity. The north wind is often associated with bad weather and could appear quite hostile, whereas the south wind is altogether gentler. But both winds do disturb; and chemically speaking they shift some of the molecules in the various spices into the wider atmosphere. The lover is inviting these winds, mindful it might disrupt her routine, because she understands the ensuing effect will be to cause the spices from her garden to be wafted abroad such that her lover can enjoy the fragrance.

More often than not, we like to feel in control and don't like our routines having to change, especially if without warning. We might see the north wind as the big disruptions in life, which may be unpleasant and unwelcome, and often come as a surprise. It can be death or suffering or major disappointment. Whatever happens, the important thing is how we are going to respond. Sometimes it leads to bitterness and resentment, a desire for revenge when people wrong us or a going into our shell to avoid repetitions etc., but it can also be an opportunity to grow character, to be a sweet-smelling savour for Christ so not only is Christ blessed but so are others. As for the petty, relatively speaking, disruptions of the south wind, it could be one of many daily irritations and annoyances that come our way from unwelcome or unexpected sources, and how we respond to these, by way of our winsome and forbearing behaviour or otherwise is how well we come through the test and whether this allows the spices to flow.

Before we leave the garden and enter the next episode in our story, we note that the lover does respond: he comes *into his garden, and eat his pleasant fruits* and again addressing his beloved as *"my sister, my spouse"* he is able to declare that *"I have gathered my myrrh with my spice; I have eaten my honeycomb with my honey; I have drunk my wine with my milk"* (5:1), making it all worthwhile.

Day 20: Knocking at the door (5:2)

"I sleep, but my heart waketh: it is the voice of my beloved that knocketh, saying, Open to me, my sister, my love, my dove, my undefiled: for my head is filled with dew, and my locks with the drops of the night."

One of the big discoveries of one's own life is, having discovered some profound truth, events conspire to test us as to how we have taken on board that truth. In our previous reading, we find the girl inviting disturbances into her life because of the good that will follow and now she is being disturbed and it is evident she does not pass the test, at least first-time round. As in 3:1 we find her on her bed resting but this time her lover is knocking at the door. He appeared to be in need with his head *filled with dew* and *locks with the drops of the night*.

This would have been even more reason to open up and let him in but this was not a convenient time, as often happens: *"I have put off my coat; how shall I put it on? I have washed my feet; how shall I defile them?"* (5:3). Not to be deterred, we read *"my beloved put in his hand by the hole of the door, and my bowels were moved for him"* (5:4). Following her reluctance, this time she does respond: *"I rose up to open to my beloved; and my hands dropped with myrrh, and my fingers with sweet smelling myrrh, upon the handles of the lock"* (5:5). But it is too late: *"I opened to my beloved; but my beloved had withdrawn himself, and was gone: my soul failed when he spake: I sought him, but I could not find him; I called him, but he gave me no answer"* (5:6) and she quickly ventures out on a search of the city in order to find her lover.

The story reminds us that true love is not limited to time and circumstances and needs to be available at all times and all circumstances, especially when there are needs, as there was then. Sadly, the girl had failed that test although she was later to get back to where she was in that relationship. We are reminded of Holman Hunt's *"Light of the World"* painting, when Christ whose head was filled with dew comes knocking at the door but it can only be opened from inside: *"Behold, I stand at the door, and knock: if any man hear my voice, and open the door, I will come in to him, and will sup with him, and he with me"* (Revelation 3:20). He is knocking at our heart's door and it could be in the guise of a person with a need or a situation needing to be sorted, not down in our diary of scheduled appointments that may govern us. We can easily do as the girl had done, putting forward plausible reasons like having just turned in, possibly after a long day when what is desired is sweet sleep but, if we are sincere about loving, we must be prepared to make sacrifices and not to act only when it is convenient.

Day 21: What is thy beloved like? (5:9)

"What is thy beloved more than another beloved, O thou fairest among women? what is thy beloved more than another beloved, that thou dost so charge us?"

We earlier left our mini saga with the girl frantically searching out her lover, having failed to open up in time after he had come knocking, and finding he had departed. For those who have experienced such intimacy, it will cause much distress finding those ties broken. She seeks her lover out. As on the previous occasion when she went into the city in search of her lover, she encounters the watchmen: "*The watchmen that went about the city found me, they smote me, they wounded me; the keepers of the walls took away my veil from me*" (5:7). The response of the watchmen this time is unsympathetic as they proceed to beat her. It reminds us of the wretched feelings and what might then follow when what was a sweet relationship has been broken by some foolish act of wilfulness on our part, including avoidable pain and even as in this case – punishment.

In desperation, she turns to the daughters of Jerusalem, ever present on the scene, who seem to know all that is going on: "*I charge you, O daughters of Jerusalem, if ye find my beloved, that ye tell him, that I am sick of love*" (5:8), but not on this occasion. They didn't have enough to go on and asked for more information. *What is thy beloved more than another beloved?* which is then repeated, is an interesting way of saying "describe him for me" or how come he's that wonderful. But even in her backslidden state they recognise something special about the girl in that they described her as *thou fairest among women* irrespective of her state at that time. She is *sick of love* and the only cure is to find her lover – thus the charge.

From a human love relationship perspective, it is worth noting if we fail to work on restoring relationships when they fail they may do so irrevocably and sadly often do. For a believer, opportunities like being asked to describe Christ may not come often but when they do we need to be ready to respond, as indeed the girl did, as we will see. The Christ we follow is not like other men, for He stands out "*as the apple tree among the trees of the wood*" (2:3). Moving as I do among those of other faiths and sometimes no faith at all, I am mindful that as a great person, prophet, teacher, leader, the historical Jesus (or myth underlying such) is often afforded much respect but the question is begged when those recognising our special love for him ask *what is thy beloved more than another beloved, that thou dost so charge us?* It might be worth pondering awhile what our response might be before finding out what the girl said, having been caught on the proverbial hop.

Day 22: White and ruddy (5:10)

"My beloved is white and ruddy, the chiefest among ten thousand."

We are still in the mini saga that began in 5:2, when the girl's lover appeared and because of her delay in responding went away, with her soon after looking for him. As she enquired, she was asked a question: *"what is thy beloved more than another beloved?"* Before meditating on the first verse in her response to that question, it is worth being reminded these words were put in the mouth of the girl by Solomon to describe himself. Given the faultless and lofty description offered that no man can ever match, one might be excused for thinking this description could not be of any mere man, even though use of superlatives are typically the language of love. We might also reflect on the words we might decide to use.

We might take this to be a description of Christ in his human form, who is *white and ruddy*. He is white because he is pure and holy and was the only man to have never sinned (which was why he alone could pay the penalty for our sin). But paradoxically he was ruddy too. As we trawl through the gospels, we see one who was the friend of sinners, the lowly, rejects and no hopers in society, who roughed it and went without, doing so joyfully with good humour, who comfortably associated with the good and the great and not so good and not so great. He knew how to *"speak a word in season to him that is weary"* (Isaiah 50:4). He is after all the Son of man and could identify with the vast array of experiences, including the disagreeable ones that may befall man, and did so willingly and ably. To use the girl's words, he is *the chiefest among ten thousand* and as such stands head and shoulders above any other, notably the best of the best, who ever lived.

Having been fired up into describing her lover, she excitedly *"speak of the things which I have made touching the king"* (Psalm 45:1), proceeding to consider the rest of his body, likening each part to something wondrous: *"His head is as the most fine gold, his locks are bushy, and black as a raven. His eyes are as the eyes of doves by the rivers of waters, washed with milk, and fitly set. His cheeks are as a bed of spices, as sweet flowers: his lips like lilies, dropping sweet smelling myrrh. His hands are as gold rings set with the beryl: his belly is as bright ivory overlaid with sapphires. His legs are as pillars of marble, set upon sockets of fine gold: his countenance is as Lebanon, excellent as the cedars. His mouth is most sweet: yea, he is altogether lovely."* (5:11-16). She is therefore able to confidently conclude *"This is my beloved, and this is my friend, O daughters of Jerusalem."* As for us, Christ is our beloved and our friend. There may be little of merit we can say concerning ourselves, but there is much we can say about Him.

Day 23: Reunited (6:2)

"My beloved is gone down into his garden, to the beds of spices, to feed in the gardens, and to gather lilies."

Before giving her amazing description of her lover's qualities, the girl had been asked *"what is thy beloved more than another beloved?"* Now, no doubt moved by her rendition of her lover, the question is changed: *"whither is thy beloved gone, O thou fairest among women? whither is thy beloved turned aside? that we may seek him with thee"* (6:1), so instead of her asking them, the Daughters of Jerusalem are now asking her, recognising again her own beauty. Not only so, but they had been won over, wanting to seek him with her. Here we have an example in how to do personal evangelism and how we might win others for Christ. We do so in part by speaking highly of the one who is *altogether lovely*.

No sooner had this question been asked than she knew the answer to her earlier question and the search and this mini adventure was ended. She could declare with confidence *"my beloved is gone down into his garden"* and given she is that garden (4:12) we find the lover back to where he belongs, with his beloved. He had returned *"to the beds of spices, to feed in the gardens, and to gather lilies"*. Once again she could declare *"I am my beloved's, and my beloved is mine: he feedeth among the lilies"* (6:3). For her this reconciliation following her distressing time apart from her lover might be translated into real time and might apply to couples when they have tiffs and need to get back together again. While hurt pride etc., may prolong estrangement, far better it is to be reconciled. Sadly, human nature being what it is, reconciling broken relationships is too often needlessly delayed. Let's be reconciled if at all possible!

When we relate the story to our own relationship with Christ, we realise we have never seen him although he is very real and should be the most significant part of our own lives. But one day we will see him and we will be with him forever but, in the meantime, we walk with him by faith, assured of his promises *"I am with you always, even unto the end of the world"* (Matthew 28:20) and *"if a man love me, he will keep my words: and my Father will love him, and we will come unto him, and make our abode with him"* (John 14:23). There will be trials and tribulations along the way and times when we may stray and fail to respond to his call, but always he is there to lovingly receive us if we return to him. The sort of intimacy enjoyed by the girl in this Song is ours to enjoy too and we too can declare to a watching and sometimes unsympathetic world *"I am my beloved's, and my beloved is mine"* and for a moment, little else seems to matter.

Day 24: An army with banners (6:4)

"Thou art beautiful, O my love, as Tirzah, comely as Jerusalem, terrible as an army with banners."

Much of this extraordinary chapter (6) is dominated by the Lover who begins by speaking highly of his beloved with whom he is fixated. Having likened her desirability to pleasant Tirzah and comely Jerusalem, describing her as *terrible as an army with banners,* he continues *"turn away thine eyes from me, for they have overcome me"* (6:5). While he re-visits familiar themes like goats' hair and sheeps' teeth, it seems from his description she has developed far beyond that of a timid, self-conscious bride and is now a formidable force in her own right. She ever remains *"my dove"*, seeing no fault in her; she is uniquely *"my undefiled is but one"* (6:9). He ends his description: *"The daughters saw her, and blessed her; yea, the queens and the concubines, and they praised her"* (6:9).

The Daughters of Jerusalem merely reinforce this view: *"Who is she that looketh forth as the morning, fair as the moon, clear as the sun, and terrible as an army with banners?"* (6:10) and *"Return, return, O Shulamite; return, return, that we may look upon thee"* (6:13). She is an object of wonder. The Lover's description is followed up: *"I went down into the garden of nuts to see the fruits of the valley, and to see whether the vine flourished and the pomegranates budded. Or ever I was aware, my soul made me like the chariots of Amminadib"* (6:11,12). While the ending is strange, almost as if ready for war, this is reinforced by *"What will ye see in the Shulamite? As it were the company of two armies"* (6:13), a veiled reference to Genesis 32:1 when Jacob along with his entourage, who with much foreboding went to meet his brother, Esau, who he had been estranged from for the past twenty years, and en-route were met by a heavenly host.

Sometimes, we may be tempted to be despondent when thinking about the state of the church, which too often appears weak, having lost its way. But also, and we are seeing more of this, the church is an object of hate and revilement, with believers suffering as a result. Looking globally, this is indeed the case. And while suffering is to be expected, the picture painted in the Bible is of a glorious church and is how it will be when Christ returns. It should inspire us on what will be and provide comfort in adversity. The church He sees is *terrible as an army with banners,* suggesting a powerful force confronting the powers of darkness, joining with the angels of God as did Jacob at Mahanaim. What we see here is what He sees (as well as those closely associated with Him) that is something glorious, and this gives us good reason from which we have good grounds for hope.

Day 25: Like a palm tree (7:7)

"This thy stature is like to a palm tree, and thy breasts to clusters of grapes."

Chapter 7:1-9 incorporates the third elaborate attempt by the Lover to describe his beloved, continuing from 4:1-15 and 6:4-9. It is again full of imagery which we note but is outside the scope of these meditations. But at least three things stand out: The growing maturity and confidence noted in chapter 6 continues. The Lover once again reveals himself as besotted with his beloved, without any reservation, and included in his description is his declaration of ardent passion. And then there is the theme of fruitfulness, which is both a priority of the Lover and as we will see (7:9-13) in the Beloved's response. This is seen, for example, in his observation: *"thy navel is like a round goblet, which wanteth not liquor: thy belly is like an heap of wheat set about with lilies"* (7:2), but we return to today's text.

The palm tree holds for the author a particular fascination. He writes this during a visit to his family in Kerala, noted for its lush greenery, which is a state in India named after palm trees, which grow there in abundance. As he mediates from the roof of the house he is staying in, which is surrounded on all sides by palm trees, although in this case the fruit is coconuts, rather than dates or grapes as per the Song it is easy to wonder at the significance of the Palm tree. One characteristic of the Palm tree is every part of the tree is useful, and this is still the case today. The fruit can be eaten raw or used as cooking ingredients. The tree itself can be used in building houses and bridges and the leaves are used in roofs of houses. Some of the fibrous material, *e.g.* surrounding the fruit, can be made into rope, and shells can be used as containers. Anything left over can be used for fuel.

We can ponder why the Lover should liken the stature of his beloved to that of a palm tree or why her breasts should be compared to clusters of grapes, although physical love making and reinforcing this picture of fruitfulness will be part of what we might invoke from this image. We might further ask why *"I will go up to the palm tree, I will take hold of the boughs thereof"* (7:8)? We may have seen people climb palm trees and have been awed by their nimble ability to do so. Clearly the lover is keen and adept in climbing, to get to the fruit. For there is little doubt the palm tree held a particular fascination for the Lover, and is mentioned as we approach the end of the description: *"now also thy breasts shall be as clusters of the vine, and the smell of thy nose like apples; And the roof of thy mouth like the best wine for my beloved"* which the Beloved does then pick up on.

Day 26: His desire is toward me (7:10)

"I am my beloved's, and his desire is toward me."

In his preceding description, the Lover ends with *"and the roof of thy mouth like the best wine for my beloved"* (7:9), to which his beloved immediately responds *"that goeth down sweetly, causing the lips of those that are asleep to speak"* and adds to it the remarkable claim *"I am my beloved's, and his desire is toward me"* (7:10), which is one of the recurring themes of this sublime Song that should warm our hearts. There appears significant progression to her earlier similar comment: *"My beloved is mine, and I am his"* (2:16) (also 6:3) but this time the emphasis is on him and not her and it is *his* desire that is toward her.

Earlier it was the Lover that was doing the initiating and convincing, inviting his beloved to join him as together they go into the great outdoors to check out how things were (2:8-13) but now it is the girl who is taking the initiative and asking him to join her so they together can sample the delights that she has laid up for him: *"come, my beloved, let us go forth into the field; let us lodge in the villages. Let us get up early to the vineyards; let us see if the vine flourish, whether the tender grape appear, and the pomegranates bud forth: there will I give thee my loves. The mandrakes give a smell, and at our gates are all manner of pleasant fruits, new and old, which I have laid up for thee, O my beloved"* (7:11,13).

Such boldness and firm intent shows how far the girl has come. But it is the reminder that now we read for the third time her making the point *"I am my beloved's"* that makes us realise his ownership is so important to her and now, without any shadow of doubt, she can say *"his desire is toward me"*. Such tender feelings are only to be expected as part of the course of true love and a reminder that in such a relationship the one belongs to the other and can rightly expect such desire to be reciprocated. Not only should this be the case at the outset, but it should be true at the end and is something all couples should keep an eye on, mindful that tests will come and we may too easily become over familiar.

What is even more amazing is that what we witness in the Song also represents the divine human relationship, as God does intend it. Firstly, from a Christian perspective, I/the Church belong to Christ and no one else. Secondly, and as incredible as it sounds and despite the number of times I/the Church may have failed Him, His desire is to toward me/His Church. When doubt and darkness beset: *"when evil thoughts molest, with this I shield my breast: may Jesus Christ be praised"* and remember: *"I am my beloved's, and his desire is toward me"*.

Day 27: Like a brother (8:1)

"O that thou wert as my brother, that sucked the breasts of my mother! when I should find thee without, I would kiss thee; yea, I should not be despised."

This may appear an unusual pick for meditation, which continues by giving the reason for the girl making her wish *"I would lead thee, and bring thee into my mother's house, who would instruct me: I would cause thee to drink of spiced wine of the juice of my pomegranate. His left hand should be under my head, and his right hand should embrace me"* (8:2,3) and repeats the charge she had made earlier not to manufacture love before its time (3:5) *"I charge you, O daughters of Jerusalem, that ye stir not up, nor awake my love, until he please"* (8:4).

It is to do with the relationship of a man and a woman, who while "in love" yet may not be married. It should be noted in the culture in which the Song is set, unlike the western culture I am more used to, notions of freedom for members of the opposite sex to mingle or make their own arrangements for marriage, let alone be physically intimate even in innocuous ways, are alien ones. It begs the question of how this particular relationship was carried out and the context for the physical intimacy that is so apparent throughout the Song. The idea of a brother sister relationship hits the right note regarding due decorum as to how the relationship should develop. It would appear, because the man was *not* her brother, any outward display of affection was not possible as it would be inappropriate, and if and when that does happen it would only rightly do so in the marriage context. We might reflect the Song is several love letters meant exclusively for each other.

For students of ancient middle eastern love poetry, the language used in the Song would likely strongly resonate with many of the sexual connotations contained throughout the Song. Our purpose is not to pontificate on a subject that has exercised many, especially in modern times, and has led many to opt for the allegorical method of interpreting the Song, embarrassed at the idea of accommodating notions of physical intimacy, but rather to make some basic points inspired by the wistful desire of the girl for the object of her affections to be like her brother. But he isn't and the time is not yet. Even if it were otherwise, it would still be necessary to practise restraint and due decorum.

We live in a culture where we are encouraged to act on our sexual urges and impulses. God is no kill joy when it comes to sex and the Song is proof. While the Song bears witness that sex is very good, there is a time and a place for sexual activity and we do well to not awaken love until the time and place is right.

Day 28: *A seal upon thine heart (8:6)*

"Set me as a seal upon thine heart, as a seal upon thine arm: for love is strong as death; jealousy is cruel as the grave: the coals thereof are coals of fire, which hath a most vehement flame."

We read earlier of the time when she observed Solomon's wedding procession (likely her own) *"who is this that cometh out of the wilderness"* (3:6) but now it is the Chorus making a similar observation about the girl *"who is this that cometh up from the wilderness, leaning upon her beloved?"* (8:5). Something remarkable has taken place since the girl's surprise encounter with the wedding procession. The two lovers are united, and coming up from the wilderness often, as far as Bible narrative goes, a place of trials and tribulations, with her in her lover's arms under his protection, and without embarrassment, for the watching world to see.

Before what is possibly the climax of the Song, comparing love and death, she remarks as one claiming her prize *"I raised thee up under the apple tree: there thy mother brought thee forth: there she brought thee forth that bare thee"*. Seals remind us of something irrevocable and legally binding and have long been in use for that purpose. As far as the beloved is concerned, she is set as a seal upon his heart and upon his arm and nothing can alter that fact, not even death. There is a finality about death and it is something none of us can escape, for that is our destiny although we hope for something beyond that. The grave will take us all and is jealous since nothing can cause us to escape its clutches. But love is more than a match for death. The love that began as an infatuation between two young lovers is no passing fad but is until death do us part. It is hot coals and a vehement flame that continues to burn brightly, regardless of death.

For a Christian believer, notably those who are passing through *the valley of the shadow of death*, there is the assurance that we have been set as a seal upon the heart of our Lord and Saviour and Lover, Jesus, and that it is a love that is as strong as death and takes us beyond the grave with the flame burning ever brightly. We will experience trials and tribulations, doubts and fears, failures and disappointments, but the whole point of the Song and, indeed, the whole Bible, is that God has ever sought to relate to his human creation as a Lover, which is nowhere seen more clearly than in the gospel narrative encapsulated in the hymn: "*Jesus, lover of my soul, Let me to Thy bosom fly, While the nearer waters roll, While the tempest still is high. Hide me, O my Saviour, hide, Till the storm of life is past; Safe into the haven guide Oh, receive my soul at last*" (Charles Wesley).

Day 29: Many waters cannot quench love (8:7)

"Many waters cannot quench love, neither can the floods drown it: if a man would give all the substance of his house for love, it would utterly be contemned."

Having asked *"set me as a seal upon thine heart, as a seal upon thine arm: for love is strong as death; jealousy is cruel as the grave: the coals thereof are coals of fire, which hath a most vehement flame"* the beloved continues to contemplate the enduring qualities of love and just as one of the harsh realities in life will be death, this is also the case with waters. As much as we may try to prepare for both, we can't anticipate how and when. We often use the illustration of much water going under the bridge in a defined period of time and by that we mean a lot will happen during that period and often the situation we see at the end is a lot different to that at the beginning for that reason. As we ponder today's text, we see that this principle aptly relates to the situations that may be found in any love relationship.

One can imagine at the outset our starry-eyed young lovers had little inkling on what would be ahead of them and it is ever thus with most such beginnings. But there will be waters and while the Beloved is confident that *many waters cannot quench love, neither can the floods drown it,* the sad reality is that all too often waters *do* quench love and lovers stop loving each other and sadly separate. The secret for staying together ought to be simple as well as profound and yet we can ponder that as much as any, it takes a lot of hard work, forgiving and forgetting, forbearing and forsaking etc. But if our text and popular love songs like *"Money can't buy me love"* are true, it is worth it, for love is a priceless gift for *if a man would give all the substance of his house for love, it would utterly be contemned.*

The challenges (waters) that come our way, whether dealing with our partners faults and foibles or facing the often harsh realities of life, we might rather avoid, that will test even the stoutest of hearts, applies as much with the relationship between the human and the divine as between humans. But it is not the intention for those waters to quench love nor for the floods to drown it. It is ever thus that *"the race is not to the swift, nor the battle to the strong, neither yet bread to the wise, nor yet favor to men of skill; but time and chance happenstance to them all"* (Ecclesiastes 9:11), and we wonder, at least as far as believers goes, if life is a testing ground aimed at refining us: *"I will refine them like silver and test them like gold"* (Zechariah 13:9). But it is back to love and our final, inevitable and unavoidable destination – death, and when it comes to waters of which there is enough to quench and drown, it is that love that will see us through it.

Day 30: The little sister (8:8)

"We have a little sister, and she hath no breasts: what shall we do for our sister in the day when she shall be spoken for?"

It is tempting when two persons consider their mutual love to look inwardly. One might come to a view that the love relationships that impress most are those that look outwardly and in particular show concern for those who are less fortunate. We are intrigued to know who the little sister referred to here is and who the brothers are who have raised the concern, and whether they are the brothers referred to in 1:6. If that were the case it would be in contrast to the callous impression we might have had when learning of the way they treated their sister. Here there is genuine concern and that is to build on the reality she has no breasts and on what is already there: *"If she be a wall, we will build upon her a palace of silver: and if she be a door, we will inclose her with boards of cedar"* (8:9). This lack of clarity as to the little sister's identity and how she relates to the girl in the Song is a quick reminder that when it comes to application we are challenged when it comes to finding the "correct" interpretation. But we can agree with the brothers that helping their sister develop her full potential is important.

The picture painted is one the girl in the Song can identify with. As she compares how she was then to now, we can see she has come a long way. *"I am a wall, and my breasts like towers: then was I in his eyes as one that found favour. Solomon had a vineyard at Baal-hamon; he let out the vineyard unto keepers; every one for the fruit thereof was to bring a thousand pieces of silver. My vineyard, which is mine, is before me: thou, O Solomon, must have a thousand, and those that keep the fruit thereof two hundred"* (8:10-12). What we do see is personal responsibility enacted. How we relate Solomon's vineyard given to the various keepers he let it out to does not appear too clear. But if the girl is one of the keepers, she is very clear what she needed to do – pay 1000 pieces of silver to Solomon, presumably as rent, and 200 pieces to them who *keep the fruit thereof*. She recognises having discharged her obligations that *my vineyard, which is mine, is before me.*

As we look to conclude our meditations on the Song, let us consider that even with the best intention and exercising due diligence in study, we won't always draw the lessons we think ought to be drawn. If there are lessons for lovers of the human and the divine, these include the need for selflessness, outwardness and responsibility, and to help those who are immature, and whatever our vineyard that we are given to attend to happens to be, we do so diligently and pay our dues.

Day 31: Make haste, my beloved (8:14)

"Make haste, my beloved, and be thou like to a roe or to a young hart upon the mountains of spices."

Now we have come to the last verse of this sublime song. These are words uttered by the Beloved in response to those previously given by the Lover: *"Thou that dwellest in the gardens, the companions hearken to thy voice: cause me to hear it"* (8:13). So we read the Lover's final parting words as he is about to be absent for likely a very long time and yearning once again to hear his beloved's voice.

Her response is swift and unequivocal. She longs for his return. We are reminded of her earlier call *"until the day break, and the shadows flee away, turn, my beloved, and be thou like a roe or a young hart upon the mountains of Bether"* (2:17). The image of the roe and the hart is invoked again, conjuring up notions of youthful vigour and the ability to confidently overcome all in its path. But the mountains of Bether have become the mountains of spices, suggesting that wherever he leaps and bounds, like a free spirit, he exudes fragrance. It is said that absence makes the heart grow fonder and so it is here as the Lover has to part, again leaving behind his beloved. But needs must and she cherishes him in her heart, eagerly awaiting his return which she hopes (*make haste*) will be soon.

We are brought back to the reason why the Song has been included in the canon of scripture. It is true that sex, love and marriage are hugely important in God's design for humankind and is sufficient reason why he wants us to be informed as to what He thinks: *"Marriage is honourable in all, and the bed undefiled"* (Hebrews 13:4) but it is also a picture of another marriage, that between Christ and the Church *"for the husband is the head of the wife, even as Christ is the head of the church: and he is the saviour of the body"* (Ephesians 5:23). While theologians will argue whether this was what was on the Holy Spirit's mind in including the Song in the Bible, the author is inclined to the belief it was and God lovers down the ages have thought so, seeing these as words of comfort.

It is difficult when considering our text *not* to think about the closing cry from the heart right at the end of our Bible: *"even so, come, Lord Jesus"* (Revelation 22:20). For those who long for the coming again of our Lord Jesus Christ, amidst a world full of sorrow and sadness and where all too often the bad guys hold sway in the affairs of men, and the good are often trodden on, that while not ignoring our responsibilities to represent Christ on the earth, and act as he would, we can longingly and expectantly say: *even so, come, Lord Jesus.*

Praying the Song

Day 1: I thank you Lord for giving us this wonderful Song. I pray as I reflect on it that you will open my eyes to see what you want me to see.

Day 2: I thank you Lord for giving me the one whose love is better than wine. I also thank you for my own beloved.

Day 3: I thank you Lord, however people may see me, I can count on your love.

Day 4: I know Lord I am far from the finished article you desire but you persist with me and want to use me to accomplish something that is glorious.

Day 5: I marvel Lord that you can always see something of worth in me.

Day 6: Thank you Lord that I may merely be a rose or a lily but I am His rose and His lily, and I have been chosen by Him.

Day 7: I thank you Lord I can sit down under Jesus' shadow and eat of His fruit.

Day 8: I rejoice Lord; I have been brought into His banqueting house, and His banner over me is love.

Day 9: I thank you Lord that all your ways are perfect and I do not need to force anything to do with love, but rather I must respond to your gracious promptings.

Day 10: I love to hear His voice Lord. I thank you He comes leaping on the mountains and there is no obstacle that he cannot deal with and overcome.

Day 11: Thank you Lord that He bids me to rise up and come away with Him.

Day 12: I am sorry Lord that I have allowed the little foxes in to destroy the vines. May I do what is necessary to take away the little foxes.

Day 13: Thank you Lord that I my beloved is mine and I am His.

Day 14: I thank you Lord, even when you seem to be far away, you are near.

Day 15: I look forward to the day Lord when I will see the King in His splendour.

Day 16: I continue to thank you Lord that you can see something of beauty in me.

Day 17: Thank you Lord you desire greatly my love.

Day 18: May I be like that garden enclosed, that is just for you Lord.

Day 19: I invite the north winds and the south winds to blow into my life Lord and welcome the pain and disturbance so the spices can flow out for you to enjoy.

Day 20: When you come knocking at my door Lord, may I be ever ready to open.

Day 21: When I have an opportunity to testify Lord, may I speak your praises.

Day 22: I thank you Lord that I can confidently say that my beloved is white and ruddy, the chiefest among ten thousand.

Day 23: O for a close walk with Thee, dear Lord.

Day 24: I am once against amazed Lord that you can see something that is of extraordinary beauty in this miserable sinner.

Day 25: May I be like that palm tree Lord – with every bit of me being of use.

Day 26: Thank you Lord that I am my beloved's, and his desire is toward me.

Day 27: Thank you Lord for that pure intimacy the beloved had with her lover.

Day 28: Thank you Lord that you have set me as a seal upon your heart and the love that we are able to share is stronger than death.

Day 29: Thank you Lord that many waters cannot quench love.

Day 30: May we ever Lord be looking out for our little sister.

Day 31: Maranatha.

Singing the Song

It is with relief and gratitude I declare my project, which began fifty years ago, as complete, although not the masterpiece I once hoped. If nothing else, it has got off my chest thoughts and insights that have come my way over the years, despite not being the definitive, all-encompassing commentary that I had once envisaged. In a strange way, what I have written, began during a one month stay with my Indian family, at our home in India, surrounded by palm trees and other examples of the natural world taken for granted in the Song, away from the distractions and amenities we take for granted back home in the UK, especially the Internet and libraries of information, may not be what I might have written a year ago or even in a year's time if I had yet again delayed "the project". There are, after all, many nooks and crannies left to explore, riches to unearth, lessons to learn, including being a better husband/wife, but I hope I can encourage any reading thus far to do just that. Here lies an important observation in the light of the thousands of commentaries that have been written about the Song of Solomon over three millennia covering a multitude of perspectives. While it is true, we need to be rightly *dividing the word of truth*, the way we see truth will depend in part on our experience of life, our circumstances, what we know already and the theology that influences us most. For this reason, I am less dismissive of those who offer something quite different to that presented here and give due credit to the valuable insights they do share.

If there has been any awakening in the fifty years I have been a Christian, it is God has sought from the outset a holy people dedicated to him with whom he can enjoy a love affair. It is meant to happen both ways and is designed to give pleasure to both God and us. The ideal man woman marriage relationship provides a picture how it should be between the human and divine. Both are important and, while keeping with tradition in emphasising the latter, sound exposition requires I don't neglect the former. Experience as well as the Song tells us relationships contain trials and tribulations, tests and challenges, to negotiate and overcome, the detail of which we cannot predict and differs for all. It is bound up in the axiom God made us for himself and we can only find rest in him – to look anywhere else only ends up as a fruitless search. God wants us exclusively for himself, and nothing else will do. Living as God wants us to, including the vexed issue of matters sexual, where many fall short of what God requires, is what the Song is mainly about, despite not mentioning God once, nor articulating this point. It is because these truths are there at the top of the pile of truths we ought to believe in and live by, that this Song is so relevant now.

The Song

Chapter 1

1 The song of songs, which is Solomon's.

Beloved

2 Let him kiss me with the kisses of his mouth: for thy love is better than wine. 3 Because of the savour of thy good ointments thy name is as ointment poured forth, therefore do the virgins love thee. 4 Draw me, we will run after thee: the king hath brought me into his chambers:

Chorus

we will be glad and rejoice in thee, we will remember thy love more than wine:

Beloved

the upright love thee. 5 I am black, but comely, O ye daughters of Jerusalem, as the tents of Kedar, as the curtains of Solomon. 6 Look not upon me, because I am black, because the sun hath looked upon me: my mother's children were angry with me; they made me the keeper of the vineyards; but mine own vineyard have I not kept. 7 Tell me, O thou whom my soul loveth, where thou feedest, where thou makest thy flock to rest at noon: for why should I be as one that turneth aside by the flocks of thy companions?

Chorus

8 If thou know not, O thou fairest among women, go thy way forth by the footsteps of the flock, and feed thy kids beside the shepherds' tents.

Lover

9 I have compared thee, O my love, to a company of horses in Pharaoh's chariots. 10 Thy cheeks are comely with rows of jewels, thy neck with chains of gold. 11 We will make thee borders of gold with studs of silver.

Beloved

12 While the king sitteth at his table, my spikenard sendeth forth the smell thereof. 13 A bundle of myrrh is my well-beloved unto me; he shall lie all night betwixt my breasts. 14 My beloved is unto me as a cluster of camphire in the vineyards of Engedi.

Lover

15 Behold, thou art fair, my love; behold, thou art fair; thou hast doves' eyes.

Beloved

16 Behold, thou art fair, my beloved, yea, pleasant: also our bed is green.

Lover

17 The beams of our house are cedar, and our rafters of fir.

Chapter 2

Beloved

1 I am the rose of Sharon, and the lily of the valleys.

Lover

2 As the lily among thorns, so is my love among the daughters.

Beloved

3 As the apple tree among the trees of the wood, so is my beloved among the sons. I sat down under his shadow with great delight, and his fruit was sweet to my taste. 4 He brought me to the banqueting house, and his banner over me was love. 5 Stay me with flagons, comfort me with apples: for I am sick of love. 6 His left hand is under my head, and his right hand doth embrace me. 7 I charge you, O ye daughters of Jerusalem, by the roes, and by the hinds of the field, that ye stir not up, nor awake my love, till he please. 8 The voice of my beloved! behold, he cometh leaping upon the mountains, skipping upon the hills. 9 My beloved is like a roe or a young hart: behold, he standeth behind our wall, he looketh forth at the windows, shewing himself through the lattice. 10 My beloved spake, and said unto me, Rise up, my love, my fair one, and come away. 11 For, lo, the winter is past, the rain is over and gone; 12 The flowers appear on the earth; the time of the singing of birds is come, and the voice of the turtle is heard in our land; 13 The fig tree putteth forth her green figs, and the vines with the tender grape give a good smell. Arise, my love, my fair one, and come away.

Lover

14 O my dove, that art in the clefts of the rock, in the secret places of the stairs, let me see thy countenance, let me hear thy voice; for sweet is thy voice, and thy countenance is comely. 15 Take us the foxes, the little foxes, that spoil the vines: for our vines have tender grapes.

Beloved

16 My beloved is mine, and I am his: he feedeth among the lilies. 17 Until the day break, and the shadows flee away, turn, my beloved, and be thou like a roe or a young hart upon the mountains of Bether.

Chapter 3

1 By night on my bed I sought him whom my soul loveth: I sought him, but I found him not. 2 I will rise now, and go about the city in the streets, and in the broad ways I will seek him whom my soul loveth: I sought him, but I found him not. 3 The watchmen that go about the city found me: to whom I said, Saw ye him whom my soul loveth? 4 It was but a little that I passed from them, but I found him whom my soul loveth: I held him, and would not let him go, until I had brought him into my mother's house, and into the chamber of her that conceived me. 5 I charge you, O ye daughters of Jerusalem, by the roes, and by the hinds of the field, that ye stir not up, nor awake my love, till he please. 6 Who is this that cometh out of the wilderness like pillars of smoke, perfumed with myrrh and frankincense, with all powders of the merchant? 7 Behold his bed, which is Solomon's; threescore valiant men are about it, of the valiant of Israel. 8 They all hold swords, being expert in war: every man hath his sword upon his thigh because of fear in the night. 9 King Solomon made himself a chariot of the wood of Lebanon. 10 He made the pillars thereof of silver, the bottom thereof of gold, the covering of it of purple, the midst thereof being paved with love, for the daughters of Jerusalem. 11 Go forth, O ye daughters of Zion, and behold

king Solomon with the crown wherewith his mother crowned him in the day of his espousals, and in the day of the gladness of his heart.

Chapter 4
Lover

1 Behold, thou art fair, my love; behold, thou art fair; thou hast doves' eyes within thy locks: thy hair is as a flock of goats, that appear from mount Gilead. 2 Thy teeth are like a flock of sheep that are even shorn, which came up from the washing; whereof every one bear twins, and none is barren among them. 3 Thy lips are like a thread of scarlet, and thy speech is comely: thy temples are like a piece of a pomegranate within thy locks. 4 Thy neck is like the tower of David builded for an armoury, whereon there hang a thousand bucklers, all shields of mighty men. 5 Thy two breasts are like two young roes that are twins, which feed among the lilies. 6 Until the day break, and the shadows flee away, I will get me to the mountain of myrrh, and to the hill of frankincense. 7 Thou art all fair, my love; there is no spot in thee. 8 Come with me from Lebanon, my spouse, with me from Lebanon: look from the top of Amana, from the top of Shenir and Hermon, from the lions' dens, from the mountains of the leopards. 9 Thou hast ravished my heart, my sister, my spouse; thou hast ravished my heart with one of thine eyes, with one chain of thy neck. 10 How fair is thy love, my sister, my spouse! how much better is thy love than wine! and the smell of thine ointments than all spices! 11 Thy lips, O my spouse, drop as the honeycomb: honey and milk are under thy tongue; and the smell of thy garments is like the smell of Lebanon. 12 A garden inclosed is my sister, my spouse; a spring shut up, a fountain sealed. 13 Thy plants are an orchard of pomegranates, with pleasant fruits; camphire, with spikenard, 14 Spikenard and saffron; calamus and cinnamon, with all trees of frankincense; myrrh and aloes, with all the chief spices: 15 A fountain of gardens, a well of living waters, and streams from Lebanon.

Beloved

16 Awake, O north wind; and come, thou south; blow upon my garden, that the spices thereof may flow out. Let my beloved come into his garden, and eat his pleasant fruits.

Chapter 5
Lover

1 I am come into my garden, my sister, my spouse: I have gathered my myrrh with my spice; I have eaten my honeycomb with my honey; I have drunk my wine with my milk:

Chorus

Eat, O friends; drink, yea, drink abundantly, O beloved.

Beloved

2 I sleep, but my heart waketh: it is the voice of my beloved that knocketh, saying, Open to me, my sister, my love, my dove, my undefiled: for my head is filled with dew, and my locks with the drops of the night. 3 I have

put off my coat; how shall I put it on? I have washed my feet; how shall I defile them? 4 My beloved put in his hand by the hole of the door, and my bowels were moved for him. 5 I rose up to open to my beloved; and my hands dropped with myrrh, and my fingers with sweet smelling myrrh, upon the handles of the lock. 6 I opened to my beloved; but my beloved had withdrawn himself, and was gone: my soul failed when he spake: I sought him, but I could not find him; I called him, but he gave me no answer. 7 The watchmen that went about the city found me, they smote me, they wounded me; the keepers of the walls took away my veil from me. 8 I charge you, O daughters of Jerusalem, if ye find my beloved, that ye tell him, that I am sick of love.

Chorus
9 What is thy beloved more than another beloved, O thou fairest among women? what is thy beloved more than another beloved, that thou dost so charge us?

Beloved
10 My beloved is white and ruddy, the chiefest among ten thousand. 11 His head is as the most fine gold, his locks are bushy, and black as a raven. 12 His eyes are as the eyes of doves by the rivers of waters, washed with milk, and fitly set. 13 His cheeks are as a bed of spices, as sweet flowers: his lips like lilies, dropping sweet smelling myrrh. 14 His hands are as gold rings set with the beryl: his belly is as bright ivory overlaid with sapphires. 15 His legs are as pillars of marble, set upon sockets of fine gold: his countenance is as Lebanon, excellent as the cedars. 16 His mouth is most sweet: yea, he is altogether lovely. This is my beloved, and this is my friend, O daughters of Jerusalem.

Chapter 6

Chorus
1 Whither is thy beloved gone, O thou fairest among women? whither is thy beloved turned aside? that we may seek him with thee.

Beloved
2 My beloved is gone down into his garden, to the beds of spices, to feed in the gardens, and to gather lilies. 3 I am my beloved's, and my beloved is mine: he feedeth among the lilies.

Lover
4 Thou art beautiful, O my love, as Tirzah, comely as Jerusalem, terrible as an army with banners. 5 Turn away thine eyes from me, for they have overcome me: thy hair is as a flock of goats that appear from Gilead. 6 Thy teeth are as a flock of sheep which go up from the washing, whereof every one beareth twins, and there is not one barren among them. 7 As a piece of a pomegranate are thy temples within thy locks. 8 There are threescore queens, and fourscore concubines, and virgins without number. 9 My dove, my undefiled is but one; she is the only one of her mother, she is the choice one of her that bare her. The daughters saw her, and blessed her; yea, the queens and the concubines, and they praised her.

Chorus
10 Who is she that looketh forth as the morning, fair as the moon, clear as the sun, and terrible as an army with banners?
Lover
11 I went down into the garden of nuts to see the fruits of the valley, and to see whether the vine flourished and the pomegranates budded. 12 Or ever I was aware, my soul made me like the chariots of Amminadib.
Chorus
13 Return, return, O Shulamite; return, return, that we may look upon thee.
Lover
What will ye see in the Shulamite? As it were the company of two armies.

Chapter 7

1 How beautiful are thy feet with shoes, O prince's daughter! the joints of thy thighs are like jewels, the work of the hands of a cunning workman. 2 Thy navel is like a round goblet, which wanteth not liquor: thy belly is like an heap of wheat set about with lilies. 3 Thy two breasts are like two young roes that are twins. 4 Thy neck is as a tower of ivory; thine eyes like the fishpools in Heshbon, by the gate of Bath-rabbim: thy nose is as the tower of Lebanon which looketh toward Damascus. 5 Thine head upon thee is like Carmel, and the hair of thine head like purple; the king is held in the galleries. 6 How fair and how pleasant art thou, O love, for delights! 7 This thy stature is like to a palm tree, and thy breasts to clusters of grapes. 8 I said, I will go up to the palm tree, I will take hold of the boughs thereof: now also thy breasts shall be as clusters of the vine, and the smell of thy nose like apples; 9 And the roof of thy mouth like the best wine for my beloved,
Beloved
that goeth down sweetly, causing the lips of those that are asleep to speak. 10 I am my beloved's, and his desire is toward me. 11 Come, my beloved, let us go forth into the field; let us lodge in the villages. 12 Let us get up early to the vineyards; let us see if the vine flourish, whether the tender grape appear, and the pomegranates bud forth: there will I give thee my loves. 13 The mandrakes give a smell, and at our gates are all manner of pleasant fruits, new and old, which I have laid up for thee, O my beloved.

Chapter 8

1 O that thou wert as my brother, that sucked the breasts of my mother! when I should find thee without, I would kiss thee; yea, I should not be despised. 2 I would lead thee, and bring thee into my mother's house, who would instruct me: I would cause thee to drink of spiced wine of the juice of my pomegranate. 3 His left hand should be under my head, and his right hand should embrace me. 4 I charge you, O daughters of Jerusalem, that ye stir not up, nor awake my love, until he please.

Chorus

5 Who is this that cometh up from the wilderness, leaning upon her beloved?

Beloved

I raised thee up under the apple tree: there thy mother brought thee forth: there she brought thee forth that bare thee. 6 Set me as a seal upon thine heart, as a seal upon thine arm: for love is strong as death; jealousy is cruel as the grave: the coals thereof are coals of fire, which hath a most vehement flame. 7 Many waters cannot quench love, neither can the floods drown it: if a man would give all the substance of his house for love, it would utterly be contemned.

Chorus

8 We have a little sister, and she hath no breasts: what shall we do for our sister in the day when she shall be spoken for? 9 If she be a wall, we will build upon her a palace of silver: and if she be a door, we will inclose her with boards of cedar.

Beloved

10 I am a wall, and my breasts like towers: then was I in his eyes as one that found favour. 11 Solomon had a vineyard at Baal-hamon; he let out the vineyard unto keepers; every one for the fruit thereof was to bring a thousand pieces of silver. 12 My vineyard, which is mine, is before me: thou, O Solomon, must have a thousand, and those that keep the fruit thereof two hundred.

Lover

13 Thou that dwellest in the gardens, the companions hearken to thy voice: cause me to hear it.

Beloved

14 Make haste, my beloved, and be thou like to a roe or to a young hart upon the mountains of spices.

The Song

Book 2

Proverbs

The way of wisdom

Introducing Proverbs

We now come to the Book of Proverbs, Solomon's second book, that precedes his third, the Book of Ecclesiastes. We follow a similar pattern to that adopted concerning the Song of Songs, with certain things worth saying that apply to each book covered in the **General Introduction.** Since Song of Songs got in first, fifty years earlier in fact, this has set the standard. I neither wish to be repetitive, nor do I propose to radically edit what I previously wrote in order to provide a slick generic introduction in order to cover all three books. I therefore beg the reader's indulgence for taking this approach, which is more about building on what went on previously, cutting to the chase (a personal challenge) and preparing needed ground work for what is the major part of what is being written about for each of the three books – thirty-one daily meditations, one for each day of the month.

Regarding authorship, we are left in no doubt, because right at the outset we read: "*The proverbs of Solomon the son of David, king of Israel*" (1:1). While not disputing whether or not Solomon wrote Proverbs (970 to 930 BC), it is nevertheless more complex than that. Some, maybe most, of the proverbs were known before Solomon, and Solomon merely did a sifting job to make these available to those who would read them later. Some proverbs are referred to as the sayings of the wise (22-24), suggesting these at least were not originated by him. Not known of course, but it would be interesting to know how many of "*three thousand proverbs*" 1 Kings 4:32 Solomon wrote ended up in the Book of Proverbs. Some 350 years later, in the reign of King Hezekiah (715 to 686 BC), others did a further editing and compiling job, perhaps removing some of the inevitable repetition Solomon had introduced in order to make what we now see set before us all the more readable. Some, maybe many, proverbs were known already in the ancient world and originated by those who were from outside of Israel, *e.g.* Egypt, including followers of gods, other than YHWH. It is perhaps a good example of common grace, that wisdom can come from unlikely sources. One may infer that part of Solomon's wisdom was to recognise the wisdom in others. We know of two named persons who contributed: Agur and Lemuel.

We also read from the outset the purpose of writing: "*To know wisdom and instruction; to perceive the words of understanding; To receive the instruction of wisdom, justice, and judgment, and equity; To give subtilty to the simple, to the young man knowledge and discretion. A wise man will hear, and will increase learning; and a man of understanding shall attain unto wise counsels: To understand a proverb, and the interpretation; the words of the wise, and their dark sayings*" (1:2-6). To complete the prologue, it is worth mentioning a statement that is central to the whole book, in that it introduces two themes repeatedly referred to: wisdom is better than foolishness and that the fear of the Lord should govern our lives: "*The fear of the Lord is the beginning of knowledge: but fools despise wisdom and instruction*" (1:7). As for the way the Book of Proverbs pans out, most would broadly agree that the following headings (as set out in my NIV Study Bible) essentially address the main break down of the book:

1. Prologue: Purpose and Theme (1:1-7)
2. The Superiority of the Way of Wisdom (1:8-9:18)
- Appeals and Warnings Confronting Youth (1:8-33)
- Commendation of Wisdom (chs. 2-4)
- Warnings against Folly (chs. 5-7)
- Appeals Addressed to Youth (chs. 8-9)
3. The Main Collection of Solomon's Proverbs (10:1-22:16)
4. The Thirty Sayings of the Wise (22:17-24:22)
5. Additional Sayings of the Wise (24:23-34)
6. Hezekiah's Collection of Solomon's Proverbs (chs. 25-29)
7. The Sayings of Agur (ch. 30)
8. The Sayings of King Lemuel (31:1-9)
9. Epilogue: The Ideal Wife (31:10-31)

A lot of the Book of Proverbs is pretty down to earth and, as one friend put it, "downright obvious". It covers all sorts of subjects, often very practical and matter of fact, and is good sound common-sense advice to help us follow the way of wisdom. Refreshingly, while God features big time, it is *not* particularly religious (which some find quite appealing) and covers all sorts of topics that could raise the eyebrows of those who are. It can be seen as advice parents (mother as well as father) would want their sons to take heed of, which given universal experience does not always happen, as lessons are often learned from the mistakes made by not taking heed of what one is taught. Proverbs was directed at men rather than women, because men were looked upon as the ones taking the lead, including in the family, although what is advised applies to us all, even today, three thousand years later, irrespective of all the cultural differences we can now see.

Interestingly, sayings from the Proverbs are not just often quoted in the NT but many find themselves being referred to in everyday life. My own experience as a preacher and hearer of many sermons is that, unlike Solomon's other books, Proverbs does not usually feature in the sermon title but is often referred to. Not only that, but in real life application, including what people write on social media, by some who are unaware they are quoting from the Bible. The English translators of Proverbs have done a creditable job given the limitations of translating breath-taking Hebrew poetry into a form that modern readers can easily identify with.

My preference for the King James Version (KJV), evidenced when we talked about the Song of Songs, continues with Proverbs, but with a caveat. While the words of the KJV are invariably lovely, they do not always do justice to giving the real meaning of the text. Not that it is the perfect solution, but I found going from the sublime to the ridiculous helped. I found to my surprise when using

The Message (MSG) and Good News (GNT) versions, alongside that of the KJV, it proved to be a fruitful approach when it came to better understanding the text.

When I wrote on the Song of Songs, it was a no brainer to dedicate this to my wife. Similarly, I would want to dedicate this book to my son, Matthew. I hope and pray he follows the wisdom set out in Proverbs, but as Solomon found out with his son, Rehoboam, there is no guarantee that it will be so, as each new generation needs to make up their mind whether they follow the way of wisdom or the way of foolishness. With this in mind, I would want to include the next generation, who because of a decay in the culture and a turning away from God, are less likely to be told about the Way of Wisdom, and in a small way these thoughts on the Book of Proverbs are my contribution to redressing the balance.

Approaching Proverbs

Coming up with thirty-one daily meditations on Proverbs is both a convenient and an inconvenient undertaking. It is convenient because, at least for seven months of the year, there are thirty-one days in the month and it readily lends itself to covering a chapter for each day, and may well encourage some readers to read through the thirty-one chapters, in Proverbs, one for each day in that month. It is inconvenient because many chapters contain miscellaneous nuggets of gold on a vast array of subjects, which one commentator compared to hundreds of fortune cookies, where the one that follows the one before is often to do with an entirely different subject, and often it would be more than stretching the point to make the connection between adjoining thoughts. Given the ideal is to provide a concise thought for the day that can somehow cover the whole chapter, it is a well-nigh impossible undertaking to do justice to everything contained in the chapter, given the vast range of subjects that are begging to be covered.

Given Solomon wrote 3000 proverbs, of which experts reckon around 500 are included within the Book of Proverbs, a better approach perhaps may be to write 365 (or 366) "thoughts for the day", *i.e.* a whole year's worth. By way of compromise, I have taken note of the main themes of Proverbs, such as those identified in the other sections, noting Solomon repeatedly returns to some of the same themes. As an approach, I have selected my texts with the view to covering the main themes and linking related texts, albeit not entirely successfully, for some nuggets may be missed altogether and my choices will inevitably reflect my own interests. I do try, though, to cross relate each day's text, usually one but sometimes more verses, to other texts to do with the same theme. I envisage readers of each day's reflection reading the whole chapter and even though I will unavoidably leave out many gems, in order to focus on the text for that day on one page, I will more often than not try to acknowledge the riches I do not cover.

The first nine chapters broadly cover certain major themes, often to do with the desirability of following the way of wisdom and the undesirability of following the way of foolishness, and there is a degree of repetition as well as urgency in the warnings, as the author returns to his main theme of going after wisdom and preoccupations like not mixing with bad company or being seduced by loose women. After Chapter 9, wise sayings, often contained in a single verse, are let rip, like bullets from a machine gun, quickly switching focus from one subject to another, and often these are not obviously related other than they are to do with the central wisdom theme. This will become marvellously obvious if readers take up my suggestion of reading a chapter a day, followed by a time of reflection.

What is so thrilling is the practicality of what is said by one who has lived long enough to have experienced life in the raw, yet given wisdom from on High to make some sort of sense of it, whether disciplining children, the value of hard work, the art of the deal, how to treat women, being honest in business, the power of the tongue, maintaining one's own counsel – and so much more. To cite my NIV Study Bible: these proverbs range widely across the broad spectrum of human situations, relationships and responsibilities; offering insights, warnings, instructions and counsels, along with frequent motivations to heed them.

In a variety of situations and relationships, the reader is exhorted to honesty, integrity, diligence, kindness, generosity, readiness to forgive, truthfulness, patience, humility, cheerfulness, loyalty, temperance, self-control and the prudent consideration of consequences that flow from attitudes, choices and/or actions. Anger should be held in check, violence and quarrelsomeness shunned, gossip avoided, arrogance repudiated. Drunkenness, gluttony, envy and greed should all be renounced. The poor are not to be exploited, the courts are not to be unjustly manipulated, legitimate authorities are to be honoured. Parents should care for the proper instruction and discipline of their children, and children should duly honour their parents and bring no disgrace on them. Human observation and experience have taught the wise that a certain order is in place in God's creation. To honour it leads to known positive effects; to defy it leads only to unhappy consequences. Life should be lived in conscious awareness of the unfailing scrutiny of the Lord and in reliance on His generous providence.

Interpreting Proverbs

Unlike with the Song of Songs, where there are two quite distinct ways of interpreting the Song that see Christian pundits going off in different directions – one a story of two lovers graphically described and the other a metaphor on how the divine and human can interact in love, such controversy does not apply to Proverbs. Even the unbeliever could affirm there is a lot of sensible stuff to be found (and often in my experience they do); readers are left in no doubt the author means what he says and says what he means and while we may see many different, valid applications, we are left in no doubt concerning what the author meant.

Sometimes Proverbs veers toward the politically incorrect and could offend a generation not used to having their sensibilities upset (although delight others who despair of a snowflake culture that discourages those who like Solomon speak as they find), or those trusting in their own righteousness, but when it comes to interpretation, we are generally left in no doubt, although the temptation of preachers to extrapolate their own ideas into the text is well nigh inevitable.

Given Proverbs is part of the inspired Word of God, I do offer the following thoughts, with a degree of trepidation … Obviously Solomon's preoccupations, implicit in his choice of words, are not necessarily my own and nor can they be, given Israel 3000 years ago is not the world I live in today and my experience and perspectives on life are not the same as Solomon's. An example at the beginning is his fixation on keeping good company and avoiding bad. This is an all too real scenario and many readers have their own examples of what happens as a result of "getting in with the wrong crowd". But to go out and murder someone in order to gain materially etc., is not a temptation most of us would ever entertain.

As to how to deal with women, we may find ourselves sexually attracted to (and it is something all too real from time immemorial), but being lured into an adulterous relationship by a loose woman is likely to be the least of our problems and, besides which, in today's culture, to see the woman as the prime instigator will usually be seen as male chauvinism. When we come to the end and consider *the wife of noble character*, while it is all good stuff, I know of few wives who include in their duties having to daily organise the household servants.

My point is, some licence is needed in our application, and a recognition of difference in culture and circumstances, and a realisation these are principles to apply and not hard and fast rules to follow and the key issue is following the way of wisdom. This is **not** the Law or the Prophets, but if we follow what is contained in these proverbs, while we cannot escape calamity, we have the wherewithal to fruitfully live our lives as God desires such that we and others will be blessed.

This is particularly pertinent if upon taking on board all the advice contained in the sayings of Solomon as the blueprint we follow in life, especially if taking a view that if we do so then life will go well for us, and then finding like Job and

Interpreting Proverbs

David, when having done all, this life does not go well. The best we should say is if we are to follow the advice of Solomon's Proverbs, we are more likely to reap the benefits, but life will not necessarily go smoothly. We need to go no further than reading Job and Solomon's Ecclesiastes sequel (as well as our own experience) for confirmation that is the case. Sometimes, fools seem to prosper and the wise suffer, at least from a temporal as opposed to an eternal perspective.

There are many examples that such is the case to be found in the Psalms. Now as then we see many examples of fools exalted and the wise abased. I don't want to get into controversy here, and I confess I have not come to a full view yet, but one difference between the OT and the NT is the former is more concerned with what goes on in this life whereas the latter is more concerned with eternity.

Yet Proverbs is worth pondering because it is so applicable for today, even if in each succeeding generation people have discovered many different applications. What is so incredible about Proverbs is it is so modern and "spot on" in its outlook, despite having been written 3000 years ago, with some of its wisdom known long before then. We may well think, what if more people had followed the advice set out in Proverbs – or, closer to home, if only I had?

Many godly people of yesteryear have impressed on earnest believers the importance of daily meditating on the Psalms as a way to approach the challenges and often disappointments of life. The same advice might be given concerning Proverbs. The cry of the heart is evident in both books as is the God who responds. In fact, if I were to commend a Bible reading pattern, ideally to cover the entire Bible in a year, I would suggest daily reading portions of Psalms and a proverb.

I for one will admit to regretting not following the profound wisdom to be found in Proverbs as much as I ought when it comes to deciding how to go about the business of daily living and making wise choices. I suspect, if I had, a lot of the pain, self-inflicted and to others, might have been avoided. Not that we can do much about our past follies but we can take note of and abide by the lessons that are set out in Proverbs, all to do with how to conduct ourselves wisely. I therefore commend the thirty-one meditations that follow, but whether readers choose to follow my train of thought or not, or indeed come up with their own set of reflections based on careful study, it matters little, but I can guarantee they will be blessed by finding the way of wisdom from carefully studying Proverbs.

Be thou my vision, O Lord of my heart
Naught be all else to me, save that thou art
Thou my best thought, by day or by night
Waking or sleeping, thy presence my light

Be thou my wisdom, and thou my true word
I ever with thee and thou with me, Lord
Thou my great Father, and I thy true son
Thou in me dwelling and I with thee one

Riches I heed not, nor vain, empty praise
Thou mine inheritance, now and always
Thou and thou only first in my heart
High King of heaven, my treasure thou art

High King of heaven, my victory won
May I reach heaven's joys, O bright heaven's sun
Heart of my own heart, whatever befall
Still be my vision, O ruler of all
Heart of my own heart, whatever befall
Still be my vision, O ruler of all

Immortal, invisible, **God only wise,**
In light inaccessible hid from our eyes,
Most blessed, most glorious, the Ancient of Days,
Almighty, victorious, Thy great name we praise.

Unresting, unhasting, and silent as light,
Nor wanting, nor wasting, Thou rulest in might;
Thy justice like mountains high soaring above
Thy clouds which are fountains of goodness and love.

To all life Thou givest, to both great and small;
In all life Thou livest, the true life of all;
We blossom and flourish as leaves on the tree,
And wither and perish, but nought changeth Thee.

Great Father of Glory, pure Father of Light
Thine angels adore Thee, all veiling their sight;
All laud we would render, O help us to see:
'Tis only the splendor of light hideth Thee.

Day 1: Fear and Wisdom (1:7)

"The fear of the Lord is the beginning of knowledge: but fools despise wisdom and instruction."

We begin our journey through Proverbs with a text relating to a theme that is referred to several times throughout the book, because it is central to what the author (Solomon) wants to say, in particular to his son, Rehoboam, who tragically failed to follow a lot of what his father had to say. Our text is the culmination of the prologue (1:1-7) of Proverbs, which after having identified the proverbs were his own then tells his reader(s) his purpose in writing, *i.e.* "*to know wisdom and instruction*" (1:2) etc. There remains a choice we all have to make: follow the way of wisdom and instruction (heeding what we are taught) or the way of the fool, which is the way not just of stupidity but of wickedness and immorality. It is worth dwelling a while on what the words our English Bibles translate as "fear", "knowledge" and "wisdom" so we are talking about the same thing:

- **Fear** (Hebrew: *yare*) can be translated by anything from respect to dread but commonly understood by learned commentators to mean reverence and awe.
- **Knowledge** (Hebrew: *yada*) goes beyond intellectually informed and includes notions of perceiving, learning, understanding, performing, and experiencing.
- **Wisdom** (Hebrew: *chokmah*) enables us to skilfully apply knowledge gained, to understand life from God's perspective and do the right thing at the right time.

As far as Solomon is concerned, the wise man does what he does out of the fear of the Lord and the foolish man does what he does ignoring the fear of the Lord and even in this chapter he gives practical examples, as in: "*my son, if sinners entice thee, consent thou not*" (1:10). He then gives a graphic example of someone being enticed by the wrong crowd, to murder an innocent person for ill-gotten gain, something that someone who truly possessed wisdom would avoid. "*Wisdom crieth without; she uttereth her voice in the streets*" (1:20) and yet it is ultimately up to the hearer whether or not he heeds that voice. The result of whether or not we decide to heed or not heed that voice is a stark one: "*For the turning away of the simple shall slay them, and the prosperity of fools shall destroy them. But whoso hearkeneth unto me shall dwell safely, and shall be quiet from fear of evil*" (1:32:33). The choice before us today therefore is whether or not we choose to fear the Lord and listen to the voice of wisdom.

Prayer: Lord help us to follow the path of wisdom and reject the path of foolishness; to do so not just because we will be better off but to honour you. We commit to you our studies in Proverbs and ask that you guide our thoughts.

Day 2: Seeking understanding (2: 3-5)

"Yea, if thou criest after knowledge, and liftest up thy voice for understanding; If thou seekest her as silver, and searchest for her as for hid treasures; Then shalt thou understand the fear of the Lord, and find the knowledge of God."

Linked with wisdom and knowledge is understanding (Hebrew: *binah*), which is more than merely accumulating information. It is about knowing the meaning of what it is that registers in our minds and the ability to correctly discern what is good or bad, desirable or undesirable, right or wrong etc. "Understand" is a word that appears 62 times in Proverbs, six times in this chapter – highlighting the important part it plays in following the right way. It should be added that all three: wisdom, knowledge, and understanding are closely associated with the fear of the Lord and do not relate to one's educational attainment or how clever we are seen to be, according to worldly standards, and is available for all who truly seek it.

What is evident from the outset is that not only is understanding worth having (more so than silver and hidden treasures) but it is something that needs to be sought after and searched for (it does not just happen) with the result: the fear and knowledge of God (2:5), wisdom, knowledge, understanding (2:6), God to be our shield (2:7), our ways are preserved (2:8), a good path to be laid out for us (2:9), there is pleasantness to the soul (2:10), we are kept in the way (2:11) and delivered from bad people (2:12). "No pain, no gain" may not quite be the figure of speech to use here, but it is likely that most do not seek and search for these things perceiving there will be pain, but if they do the gain is more than worth it. As for the bad people (the fools) that the wise and understanding are to be delivered from and as far as possible, avoid, Solomon was in no doubt where they are heading and, with them, those who do not do what he says: darkness (2:13), perverseness (2:14), crookedness (2:15).

And then there is the *forbidden woman* (2:16) (a theme he is to return to again and again) warning of the dire results of falling into her clutches, for "*none who go to her come back, nor do they regain the paths of life*" (2:19). He summarises what happens taking either path: "*For the upright shall dwell in the land, and the perfect shall remain in it. But the wicked shall be cut off from the earth, and the transgressors shall be rooted out of it*" (2:21,22). The challenge facing us is which path will we take and how desirous are we to seek after the way of wisdom, knowledge and understanding?

Prayer: Thank you Lord for showing us that knowledge and understanding is something worth seeking out and searching for and in so doing we find treasure and what truly matters in life. May we be those who make this our priority.

Day 3: Trust in the Lord (3:5,6)

"Trust in the Lord with all thine heart; and lean not unto thine own understanding. In all thy ways acknowledge him, and he shall direct thy paths."

Proverbs is full of memorable quotes that often crop up in sermons or when one person exhorts another, and our text today could well be at the top of the list. Our text is wedged between two related thoughts: the benefits that follow from keeping God's commands (3:1-4) and the blessings that ensue when we put God first in our lives (3:7-10). Our text is one that we can refer to every day as it always applies. But first, let us break down our text into four components:

Trust in the Lord – the exhortation to trust the Lord as opposed to ourselves, anyone or anything else, is repeated many times in the Bible, but the reality is that too often there is a "but" as to why we do not do what we are told is right.

Lean not unto thine own understanding – the natural human tendency is for ourselves to be the key to getting understanding, which as we discussed earlier is something desirable. The message here is clear – it ought to be Him, not us.

In all thy ways acknowledge him – we also tend often to forget or ignore the Lord in the plethora of activities that occupy us in life, and that is a mistake. It would be true to say that the more we acknowledge Him the more He blesses.

He shall direct thy paths – we need to be guided throughout our journey in life, easy and hard, big and small, right now and long term. The climax of our text is that if we do what is required of us, He will direct us concerning the right path.

As far as material for meditation, in this, as in many chapters, we are spoilt for choice, and some of the thoughts we do not elaborate on now will crop up in later chapters and we will look at them then, but in case we do not, we set a marker here. The following then are some texts, relevant for today and worth pondering:

1. *"Be not afraid of sudden fear, neither of the desolation of the wicked, when it cometh"* (v25).
2. *"Withhold not good from them to whom it is due, when it is in the power of thine hand to do it"* (v27).
3. *"Envy thou not the oppressor, and choose none of his ways"* (v31).
4. *"He scorneth the scorners: but he giveth grace unto the lowly"* (v34).

Prayer: We thank you Lord it is ever your desire to direct our paths and that is true for the big and hard choices we have to make as well as the small and easy ones. Today, may we put our trust in you as, above all, we want to please you.

Day 4: Guard your heart (4:23)

"Keep thy heart with all diligence; for out of it are the issues of life."

Before we attend to our verse for the day, it is worth recapping the earlier part of the chapter, which is repeating and reinforcing what has already been said, particularly the paramount importance of getting wisdom and understanding, and avoiding the path of the wicked and evil men, and what happens (whether blessing or cursing, life or death, honour or shame) if we, or specifically the son Solomon was trying to influence, choose or not the way of wisdom: *e.g. "Exalt her, and she shall promote thee: she shall bring thee to honour, when thou dost embrace her"* (4:8). Wisdom is referred to (as in chapter 3) as "she", something we will return to later when we find a whole chapter that is devoted to Lady Wisdom. We are also reminded here of the importance of the heart, *e.g. "let them not depart from thine eyes; keep them in the midst of thine heart"* (4:21). "Heart" is referred to 82 times in Proverbs in a large array of different contexts.

The word's first appearance is *"so that thou incline thine ear unto wisdom, and apply thine heart to understanding"* (2:2). "Heart" (Hebrew *lebab*) occurs 724 times in the Old Testament, indicating its importance as that which determines how we respond to or determine what to do on our life's journey. It denotes a person's centre for both physical and emotional-intellectual-moral activities. In the ancient world, the heart represented the origin of our thoughts and centre of our being. The Great Command includes loving YHWH with all our heart, and it is our heart that he desires. Not always realised, but a large section of the Hebrew scriptures is poetry, where God is speaking from His heart and poetry best conveys His feelings.

Two modern renditions of our text are *"keep vigilant watch over your heart; that's where life starts"* and *"be careful how you think; your life is shaped by your thoughts"*. The heart is where our choice of everything we do, think, say, sense, feel etc., begins. Entertaining harmful thoughts, opinions, influences, habits, decisions etc., draws us away from God's path, onto the slippery slope that leads to destruction. Besides pursuing wisdom with all diligence, we should be guarding our heart. Our chapter ends urging us to follow the straight path and not to turn from it. *"Let thine eyes look right on, and let thine eyelids look straight before thee. Ponder the path of thy feet, and let all thy ways be established. Turn not to the right hand nor to the left: remove thy foot from evil"* (4:24-27).

Prayer: We thank you Lord for your words of life. May they not just be in our heads but in our hearts too. We thank you for reminding us of the importance of keeping our heart with all diligence, since from it flows the springs of life. Thank you for the grace to do so. May we be those who love you with all our hearts.

Day 5: *The loving deer (5:18,19)*

"Let thy fountain be blessed: and rejoice with the wife of thy youth. Let her be as the loving hind and pleasant roe; let her breasts satisfy thee at all times; and be thou ravished always with her love."

In exhorting his son to pay attention to wisdom and listen carefully to counsel, Solomon brings up the matter of the loose, predatory woman, whose clutches he needs to avoid. Sexual immorality, while one of many sins we can fall into, is all too prevalent and alluring in our culture and manifests itself in many ways, as well as there being many ways we can yield to the temptation of sexual sin. We have here just one example of many, where we can go astray, as is often borne out by experience, even among those we least expect, with tragic results. We are told: "*Do not love the world or anything in the world ... For all that is in the world, the lust of the flesh, and the lust of the eyes, and the pride of life*" 1John 2:15,16; also "*flee sexual immorality*" 1 Corinthians 6:18 and "*youthful lusts*" 2 Timothy 2:22.

If there is a remedy to falling into sexual temptation, it is instruction (translated as discipline too) (Hebrew: *musar*). "*For lack of discipline they will die, led astray by their own great folly*" (NIV 5:23). Then we are told: "*Drink waters out of thine own cistern, and running waters out of thine own well. Let thy fountains be dispersed abroad, and rivers of waters in the streets. Let them be only thine own, and not strangers with thee. Let thy fountain be blessed: and rejoice with the wife of thy youth*" (5:15-18). While marriage is not for everyone, and is not without challenges, *e.g.* if a wife is "*disgraceful*" (12:4), "*quarrelsome*" (19:3), "*nagging*" (21:19), men who are married need be faithful to their wife, cherish and delight in her, resist temptation to sexual immorality, and to be wise!

Solomon does not shy away from the importance of sexuality and pleasure, as seen in his Song of Songs. A husband should picture his wife as a loving hind (deer) and a graceful doe. He should be intoxicated by her love. Proverbs, like the Song, shows that God considers physical attraction and conjugal love within a marriage as beautiful and commendable. The difference between sexual love in marriage and sensual lust in adultery is striking. The former is lifelong and satisfying; the latter is momentary and destructive. God instituted marriage between a man and a woman as a lifelong, loving partnership. When an adulterer breaks the bond of that partnership, pain and remorse fill his soul. Solomon's fixation on marital fidelity is perhaps one of many great examples of his wisdom.

Prayer: We thank you Lord for the gift of marriage and, for those of us who are married, our spouses. Help us to be good husbands and wives and to resist the temptation of breaking our marriage vows. Cleanse us all from any impurity.

Day 6: Go to the ant (6:6)

"Go to the ant, thou sluggard; consider her ways, and be wise."

Proverbs, as we see and will see more of, is refreshingly, irreligiously, practical and totally down to earth. Our chapter begins with a warning against putting up security for a friend's debt and the need to get out of that arrangement (6:1) and later the danger of looking to bad people, however enticing (6:12-15), and seven short sharp sayings of things the Lord hates: *"A proud look, a lying tongue, and hands that shed innocent blood, An heart that deviseth wicked imaginations, feet that be swift in running to mischief, A false witness that speaketh lies, and he that soweth discord among brethren"* (6:17-18), ending with warnings of what happens to the thief and adulterer. In today's thought: we will consider the ant.

Ants are great teachers (30:24-28). As a natural history buff, Solomon would have seen and derived many lessons for life. Ants are diligent, by working hard without coercion, and prudent by saving part of all production. This in contrast with a sluggard, a person who is slow, lazy, and does not like to work hard. He is a pain and risk to those that must rely on him (10:26). Diligent men, or those that work hard, will be successful (10:4; 12:24; 14:23; 22:29; 28:19), but lazy men, who avoid hard work, ultimately lose out (6:10-11; 12:24; 19:15; 20:4,13; 24:30-34). Sluggards are too arrogant to be taught (26:16). They stay in bed, for they love sleep (6:9-11; 20:13; 24:30-34). They have energy to turn back and forth in bed, but not to get food to their mouths (26:14-15). They want the good things of life like others, but they do not want to work for them (13:4).

Ants have an excellent work ethic, unlike sluggards. They get up, get to work, and stay at work. They are always moving, quickly and energetically. They work efficiently, tirelessly and fast. They do not stand around, sit around, or drag through their work. They do not pace themselves to spread work out: they go right to the core of a project and work hard until it is finished. They will not quit until the job is done. They do not need supervision (6:7), for they find something to do without direction. When times are good, they work hard to store up for bad times (6:8); they do not take it easy because there is the appearance of plenty. They store surplus rather than eat it all. They deny short-term pleasure for long-term prosperity. They help their colony to succeed. They are unselfish. They do not choose the easiest way or get discouraged. When facing difficulties, they try again until successful. They travel great distances to find their food. The lesson is obvious – let us be like the ant!

Prayer: Thank you Lord for the example of the ant. May we follow this rather than that of the sluggard. There is so much that needs to be done here on planet earth and we need to be smart, diligent and hard working. Help us to do that.

Day 7: Keep God's commands (7:1)

"My son, keep my words, and lay up my commandments with thee."

Proverbs is full of wisdom relating to many different aspects of life. Slightly frustrating trying to cover all of these, when some seem more pertinent than Solomon's obsession with immoral women, for yet again Solomon devotes the majority of this chapter to a theme he has already done, so it seems, to proverbial death – that of the lustful, predatory woman intent on seducing *"my son"* using crafty flattery. Ours is not to argue why the Bible emphasises certain things more than others and the truth is that sexual immorality has ruined many. Such scenarios are clearly important as he lays out how the woman entraps and the gullibility of the man along with his fate, which is *"the way to hell"* (1:27), when he succumbs. We might also infer that sexual sin in all sorts of guises has a similar outcome. It is why, as pointed out earlier, we need our own intimate relationship with wisdom and understanding and the need: *"to say unto wisdom, Thou art my sister; and call understanding thy kinswoman"* (7:4) to prevent this, for by doing so we find the way of life as opposed to that of death. While we title our thought: *"**keeping God's commands**"*, as far as Solomon was concerned, they are *my* (i.e. his commands) and his words, reminding us of the need to take heed of wise counsel, primarily a parental responsibility, but also from those who are wise.

Keeping these commands is important, and we must treasure them greatly: *"keep my commandments, and live; and my law as the apple of thine eye"* (7:2). We are told: *"Bind them upon thy fingers, write them upon the table of thine heart"* (7:3), reminding us how the Children of Israel were expected to treat the Law God gave Moses: *"And these words, which I command thee this day, shall be in thine heart: And thou shalt teach them diligently unto thy children, and shalt talk of them when thou sittest in thine house, and when thou walkest by the way, and when thou liest down, and when thou risest up. And thou shalt bind them for a sign upon thine hand, and they shall be as frontlets between thine eyes"* Deuteronomy 6:8. While, as New Testament people, we are under grace, not law, doing the right thing as God sets it out is of paramount importance. Taking heed to what is God's blueprint for living our lives should be that of *the apple of thine eye* and these "commands" should be bound to our fingers and written on our hearts. We ought to concur with the Psalmist and act accordingly: *"With my whole heart have I sought thee: O let me not wander from thy commandments"* Psalm 119:10.

Prayer: We thank you for your commands Lord, which are for our own good, to obey. We are sorry when we break them. May we greatly desire wisdom and understanding and treasure your commands so we keep on the straight path.

Day 8: Wisdom cries out (8:1)

"Doth not wisdom cry? and understanding put forth her voice?"

A dominant theme of these early chapters is of the all too prevalent lure of sin, in contrast to the call of wisdom, yet it can be countered by wisdom: violence and protection (ch. 1); perverseness and righteousness (ch. 2); arrogance and humility (ch. 3); darkness and light (ch. 4); adultery and marital love (ch. 5); laziness and diligence (ch. 6); sexual temptation and purity (ch. 7). All this is covered, and much else besides, in wisdom's cry, which is loud and open and to all persons, high and low, and the result of which is fruit that lasts a lifetime.

As for Lady Wisdom, in contrast to that which is sin: "*my mouth shall speak truth; and wickedness is an abomination to my lips. All the words of my mouth are in righteousness; there is nothing froward or perverse in them. They are all plain to him that understandeth, and right to them that find knowledge. Receive my instruction, and not silver; and knowledge rather than choice gold. For wisdom is better than rubies; and all the things that may be desired are not to be compared to it*" (8:7-11). As for wisdom's rewards: "*I love them that love me; and those that seek me early shall find me … My fruit is better than gold, yea, than fine gold; and my revenue than choice silver … That I may cause those that love me to inherit substance; and I will fill their treasures.*" (8:17,19, 21). Then what may come as a surprise, yet important in establishing the value of wisdom, is a section that takes us way back to the beginning of time: "*The Lord possessed me in the beginning of his way, before his works of old. I was set up from everlasting, from the beginning, or ever the earth was*" (8:22,23). We then read about the various acts of creation, and we note always wisdom was there: "*I was by him, as one brought up with him: and I was daily his delight, rejoicing always before him; Rejoicing in the habitable part of his earth; and my delights were with the sons of men*" (8:30,31). We are told (John 1:1-3) Jesus was with God in the beginning and He is also wisdom: "*Christ the power of God, and the **wisdom** of God*" 1 Corinthians 1:24 and "*In whom are hid all the treasures of **wisdom** and knowledge*" Colossians 2:3. This chapter ends, reminding us of the stark choice facing us all, either by finding wisdom or rejecting it: "*For whoso findeth me findeth life, and shall obtain favour of the Lord. But he that sinneth against me wrongeth his own soul: all they that hate me love death*" (8:35,36).

Prayer: We thank you Lord Jesus you are the wisdom of God, who was there in the beginning. We thank you wisdom is ever crying out and can be found by the least of us. We thank you for the rich rewards given to those who find wisdom. May it be that we continually walk in the path of wisdom and reject that of sin.

Day 9: Reprove not a scorner (9:8,9)

"Reprove not a scorner, lest he hate thee: rebuke a wise man, and he will love thee. Give instruction to a wise man, and he will be yet wiser: teach a just man, and he will increase in learning."

Before we turn to the "Proverbs of Solomon", Chapter 10 onwards, which is an assortment of short, pithy quotes, skilfully covering many subjects from the sublime to the ridiculous, without pious gobbledegook, we round off these earlier chapters that are to do primarily with wisdom and understanding, and the importance of fearing the Lord and knowing Him, encapsulated in one of the most memorable of all the proverbs: *"The fear of the Lord is the beginning of wisdom: and the knowledge of the holy is understanding"* (9:10). We are told at the start of our chapter *"wisdom hath builded her house"* (9:1). She is inviting all and sundry to dine at her house, notably those confused about life, and not knowing what's going on, and for them to leave their impoverished confusion and live.

Try as best we may, persuading people to follow the right path will work with some but not all. We are told if we try to reason with an arrogant cynic, we will effectively get slapped in the face and, when we confront bad behaviour, a similar outcome. The moral is not to waste time on a scoffer as all we will get for our pains is abuse. But if we correct those who care about life, that is a different proposition: they will love us for it. The moral is to save our breath for the wise and they will be wiser. We should tell them what we know and they will profit. The lesson is that skilled living gets its start in the fear of God and insight into life from knowing a Holy God. It is through Lady Wisdom that our lives deepen, and the years of our lives ripen. The choice is a stark one and one we all need to make: live wisely and wisdom will permeate your life; mock life and life will mock you. Being told we are wrong is never easy and neither is receiving counsel that takes us out of our comfort zone, but if we want to be truly just and wise then we know what to do. We conclude this section of Proverbs by returning to an often-repeated theme, that of a predatory, immoral woman trying to entice the foolish man, who may well be going about his regular business, to do the wrong thing. *"Stolen waters are sweet, and bread eaten in secret is pleasant"* (9:17) may appear an attractive proposition, but consider where going down that path ends: *"he knoweth not that the dead are there; and that her guests are in the depths of hell"* (9:18).

Prayer: We thank you for the wonderful truth that the fear of the Lord is the beginning of wisdom, and the knowledge of the holy is understanding. May we be those who seek after wisdom and righteousness; to receive instruction to be wiser, and teaching to add to knowledge, so that in all things we may honour you.

Day 10: A wise son (10:1)

"The proverbs of Solomon. A wise son maketh a glad father: but a foolish son is the heaviness of his mother."

As we begin to break down "the proverbs of Solomon", it is worth bearing in mind two related themes. The first is the pre-occupation of the father (and mother too) to instil wisdom in his son (a lesson all parents should heed). Proverbs has a lot to say on hopes for and expectations of sons and bringing up children, which we will return to. For now, consider this practical, consequential aspect: *"he that gathereth in summer is a wise son: but he that sleepeth in harvest is a son that causeth shame"* (10:5). Our second theme is the notion of "righteous", which is the hallmark of how a son should live his life from that point on, and is something those of us who are Christian parents might and should want for our children to be. The words "righteousness" (Hebrew *tsedaqah*), "righteous" (Hebrew *tsaddiq*) carry with them the meaning of blameless, innocence, justice, ethical conduct, and are important attributes of God and His expectation for people. The words appear 510 times in the Bible, 75 times in Proverbs and 10 times in this chapter, all in a positive context, such that we are left in no doubt as to its importance:

1. *Treasures of wickedness profit nothing: but **righteousness** delivereth from death* (10:2).
2. *The Lord will not suffer the soul of the **righteous** to famish: but he casteth away the substance of the wicked* (10:3).
3. *The mouth of a **righteous** man is a well of life: but violence covereth the mouth of the wicked* (10:11).
4. *The labour of the **righteous** tendeth to life: the fruit of the wicked to sin* (10:16).
5. *The lips of the **righteous** feed many: fools die for want of wisdom* (10:21).
6. *The fear of the wicked, it shall come upon him: but the desire of the **righteous** shall be granted* (10:24).
7. *As the whirlwind passeth, so is the wicked no more: but the **righteous** is an everlasting foundation* (10:25).
8. *The hope of the **righteous** shall be gladness: but the expectation of the wicked shall perish* (10:28).
9. *The **righteous** shall never be removed: but the wicked shall not inhabit the earth* (10:30).
10. *The lips of the **righteous** know what is acceptable: but the mouth of the wicked speaketh frowardness* (10:32).

Prayer: Thank you Lord for sons. Those of us who are parents, help us to bring them up well. Those of us who are sons, may we act wisely and righteously.

Day 11: The liberal soul (11:25)

"The liberal soul shall be made fat: and he that watereth shall be watered also himself."

Or *"Whoever brings blessing will be enriched, and one who waters will himself be watered"* (ESV) or *"A generous person will be prosperous, and one who gives others plenty of water will himself be given plenty"* (NASB) or *"Yes, the liberal man shall be rich! By watering others, he waters himself"* (Living Bible). *"The one who blesses others is abundantly blessed; those who help others are helped"* (MSG). Selecting a text of the day from many wonderful texts is a nigh impossible task. We are confronted with right on target truths, *e.g.* maintaining a fair balance (11:1), with pride comes shame (11:2), why we shouldn't trust in riches (11:4). We can go on with the gems found in the next 27 verses. The importance of righteousness, which we identified in the previous chapter, continues to be referred to (12 times in chapter 11). It delivers from death (11:4); keeps us in the straight way (11:5) and delivers the upright (11:6).

As we reflect on today's text, we are hit wonderfully hard with the importance of having a generous spirit, the desire of which is to give and not to withhold. Human nature being the way it is, we can easily be generous to some and not others or choose the time or circumstances in which we can show generosity or liberality or simply bless others. But the truly liberal man is not so constrained and will use whatever opportunity he has to be a blessing to other people and, come to think of it, it might be something we should all consider in our dealings with people, even those we may feel not obligated to or naturally drawn toward. While our acting in this way should be its own reward, we receive an additional reward promised here: *"he that watereth shall be watered also himself"*.

If there is a moral, it is we can do so knowing that we cannot out give or out bless God. Interesting are the verses before our text, indicating this attitude of liberality is a culmination of righteous living: *"The desire of the righteous is only good: but the expectation of the wicked is wrath. There is that scattereth, and yet increaseth; and there is that withholdeth more than is meet, but it tendeth to poverty"* (11:23,24), as well as the verse to follow, which reminds us of what happens if our attitude in not generous: *"He that withholdeth corn, the people shall curse him: but blessing shall be upon the head of him that selleth it"* (11:26). We end our chapter reminded again of the stark choice: *"The fruit of the righteous is a tree of life; and he that winneth souls is wise. Behold, the righteous shall be recompensed in the earth: much more the wicked and the sinner"* (11:30,31).

Prayer: May we be generous people Lord, who live our lives such that we can be a blessing to other people. We thank you that you bless the liberal soul.

Day 12: Heaviness of heart (12:25)

"Heaviness in the heart of man maketh it stoop: but a good word maketh it glad."

There are two key aspects to our text for today: the recognition of depression and how it can bring us down (*worry weighs us down*) and what is the ideal antidote: a timely word of encouragement that can lift us up (*a cheerful word picks us up*). As for having the blues or being depressed, it is a common human experience, and the last thing we should be doing is to tell people to pull themselves together. We can perhaps identify, for example, with the Psalmist, who was able to say: *"why art thou cast down, O my soul? and why art thou disquieted in me? hope thou in God: for I shall yet praise him for the help of his countenance"* Psalm 42:5. Just as a heart can be made heavy (for whatever reason and the reasons are many), so one way to lift someone out of depression is a good word, as with the Servant, who we often identify with Jesus, who could and did give to those in need: *"The Lord God hath given me the tongue of the learned, that I should know how to speak a word in season to him that is weary: he wakeneth morning by morning, he wakeneth mine ear to hear as the learned"* Isaiah 50:4.

The powerful effect of the spoken word, linked the tongue, is a recurring theme in Proverbs: *"He that speaketh truth sheweth forth righteousness: but a false witness deceit. There is that speaketh like the piercings of a sword: but the tongue of the wise is health. The lip of truth shall be established for ever: but a lying tongue is but for a moment ... Lying lips are abomination to the Lord: but they that deal truly are his delight* (12:17-19, 22). It is a sobering thought our tongue, which can do so much good, such as lifting up the downcast, can also do much harm and is something we need to guard: *"It only takes a spark, remember, to set off a forest fire. A careless or wrongly placed word out of your mouth can do that. By our speech we can ruin the world, turn harmony to chaos, throw mud on a reputation, send the whole world up in smoke and go up in smoke with it, smoke right from the pit of hell. This is scary: You can tame a tiger, but you can't tame a tongue - it's never been done. The tongue runs wild, a wanton killer. With our tongues we bless God our Father; with the same tongues we curse the very men and women he made in his image. Curses and blessings out of the same mouth!"* (James 3:5-9 MSG.) Other gems include: delighting in God (12:2), being rooted in God (12:3), a good wife (12:4), talking sense (12:8), good to be ordinary (12:9), kindness to animals (12:10), staying on the job (12:11), righteous give life (12:12)

Prayer: We recognise we all can be downhearted and there are many things that might dampen our spirits. Lord, help us to see it in others so we may be those who bring a timely word of blessing. Help us to say the right things at the right time.

Day 13: When to keep quiet (13:3)

"He that keepeth his mouth keepeth his life: but he that openeth wide his lips shall have destruction."

Our first thought is to continue where we left off yesterday, about the power of the tongue. In our text, it is more than implied that it may well go better for us if we say little: *"self-control means controlling the tongue! A quick retort can ruin everything"*. We may all look back with regret when we said something when it was better to say nothing. The moral is: a few well-chosen words are better than many that aren't. We want to speak when we think we have something needful to say but, if we do, we should adopt the true, necessary and kind principle and ask three questions: is what we say factually correct; do we really need to say it and does it lift people up rather than put them down? We do well to remember: *"let not thine heart be hasty to utter anything before God: for God is in heaven, and thou upon earth: therefore let thy words be few"* Ecclesiastes 5:2.

For our second thought, we are reminded of the importance of hope: *"Hope deferred maketh the heart sick: but when the desire cometh, it is a tree of life"* (13:12). Few can live comfortably if hope, whatever it happens to be in, is absent. Our motive to live is having hope and, for Christians, it includes the coming again of Christ and the life to come. But in our text, hope is delayed, indefinitely perhaps, and as a result the seat of our emotions, our heart, is sick. True to his lack of moralising, Solomon does not identify where our hopes ought to lie. He merely points out the consequences when hope is or isn't forthcoming.

Our third thought returns to a theme often touched on: *"Train up a child in the way he should go: and when he is old, he will not depart from it"* (22:6). Another memorable but controversial text is: *"He that spareth his rod hateth his son: but he that loveth him chasteneth him betimes"* (13:24). Beating a naughty child does not sit well in today's culture. It is not our intention to say if and when to apply such punishment. It is noted that no-one who has children brings them up 100% perfectly and for some parents it is far lower than that. But it might equally be observed that unruly behaviour in a child, that might well extend into adulthood, is often a result of a lack of parental discipline. Solomon was, as we have noted earlier, a failed father, given what we know about his son, Rehoboam. He knew what he needed to do and, while we can't score his parenting record, we can say Solomon did at least offer sound advice that all parents would do well to apply.

Prayer: Help us Lord to speak only when we need to. When we do, help us say the right thing in the right way. Help us be good parents bringing up our children.

Day 14: A way which seems right (14:12)

"There is a way which seemeth right unto a man, but the end thereof are the ways of death."

Before we consider three texts, including the above, let us first revisit three related themes, key to understanding Proverbs and specifically as related to our three texts: righteousness, wisdom and the fear of the Lord; for example *"Every wise woman buildeth her house: but the foolish plucketh it down with her hands. He that walketh in his uprightness feareth the Lord: but he that is perverse in his ways despiseth him. In the mouth of the foolish is a rod of pride: but the lips of the wise shall preserve them"* (14:1-3) and *"The wisdom of the prudent is to understand his way: but the folly of fools is deceit. Fools make a mock at sin: but among the righteous there is favour"* (14:8,9). It is worth bringing in here the parable of Jesus of the wise and foolish builders Matthew 7:24-27. There are two categories: the wise and foolish, and it poses the question, which one are we in? It matters, because humankind likes to think its actions are right, and often proudly says so, but this belief can turn out as wrong, even to the point of death.

Our second text relates to the way we treat the poor. While at the bottom of the societal heap such can easily invite mistreatment, with little to repay those who show them compassion, the righteous, wise, God fearers are those who should step in. There may be nothing in it for them, other than doing right. *"He that oppresseth the poor reproacheth his Maker: but he that honoureth him hath mercy on the poor"* (14:31). We are also told: *"The poor is hated even of his own neighbour: but the rich hath many friends. He that despiseth his neighbour sinneth: but he that hath mercy on the poor, happy is he"* (14:20,21). Day to day observance reveals many opportunities to bless the poor. We should continue to show mercy, and this may put to shame those who don't.

Our third text is *"Righteousness exalteth a nation: but sin is a reproach to any people"* (14:34). It provides an important reason why righteousness is needed – it makes a country strong, and why sin is a bad thing – it leaves the people weak. We might lament, especially if living in lands with a rich Judaeo-Christian heritage, when God's law is (increasingly) rejected and the unrighteous often call the tune. An example of societal wickedness is aborting babies. The righteous may want their country to turn to righteousness, adopt righteous laws and practices and be governed by righteous people, but such expectation may be unrealistic, yet if sin is endorsed people suffer. Our task is being exemplars of righteousness and praying as such.

Prayer: Lord, may righteousness, wisdom and the fear of you feature highly in how we live life, as we make plans, care for the poor and intercede for our nation.

Day 15: A soft answer (15:1)

"A soft answer turneth away wrath: but grievous words stir up anger."

Are we feeling challenged and uplifted as we reach the half-way point in our journey through Proverbs? We should be as we meditate and one verse after another jumps out of the pages, combining down to earthiness and up in the cloudiness, as profound truth strikes to the core. Today we revisit two key themes: the use of the tongue and the fear of the Lord, while doing our customary injustice to a lot else besides that might help us in our journey along the way of wisdom. There is an all too human propensity to let rip our righteous indignation with a piece of our mind (invariably manifesting itself through the use of our tongue). Solomon shows us a better way: *"A gentle response defuses anger, but a sharp tongue kindles a temper-fire"* (15:1 MSG). How often might we look back when a few well-chosen words gently spoken, let us say in a spirit of reconciliation and grace, calmed what could have become a fraught and acrimonious situation and when doing the opposite made things worse. This is not a lecture on how to be meek and mild, for as Solomon tells us elsewhere, there is: *"a time to keep silence, and a time to speak"* Ecclesiastes 3:7, but he lays down an important principle that more often than not, in awkward situations, we would do well to adopt. As for the use of the tongue, consider: *"The tongue of the wise useth knowledge aright: but the mouth of fools poureth out foolishness … A wholesome tongue is a tree of life: but perverseness therein is a breach in the spirit … The lips of the wise disperse knowledge: but the heart of the foolish doeth not so"* (15:2,4,7).

Just as with the use of the tongue, there is more profound truth associated with the notion of the fear of the Lord, for example when we are told having little of this world's goods with the fear of the Lord is better than having a lot without that fear, reminding us of texts like: *"godliness with contentment is great gain"* (1 Timothy 6:6). *"Better is little with the fear of the Lord than great treasure and trouble therewith. Better is a dinner of herbs where love is, than a stalled ox and hatred therewith"* (15:16,17). The remainder of the chapter paints a picture of a wise, righteous, peace loving, thoughtful man, who is ever seeking wisdom, open to reproof and instruction, content with the little he has but confident that the Lord hears his prayers, unlike the foolish, proud, greedy, wicked man who does the very opposite, whose end is ignominious. The chapter concludes: *"The fear of the Lord is the instruction of wisdom; and before honour is humility"* (15:33).

Prayer: Help us to be content with the little we have and prioritise what matters as we fear you O Lord. Help us in the use of our tongues by saying the right words in the right spirit, always seasoned with salt, seeking humility before honour.

Day 16: Pride comes before a fall (16:18)

"Pride goeth before destruction, and an haughty spirit before a fall."

Also *"Better it is to be of an humble spirit with the lowly, than to divide the spoil with the proud"* (16:19). "Pride comes before a fall" is one saying often found in every day speech, with people often not realising it originated in Proverbs. But before we reflect on the matter of pride, we are reminded, as is often Solomon's wont, before landing us with a particular gem, he precedes it by "better is it" advice, and of the ground earlier covered, including the part wisdom, by which we should live our lives, plays, as well as to put us humbly and soundly in our place. *"Mortals make elaborate plans, but God has the last word. Humans are satisfied with whatever looks good; God probes for what is good. Put God in charge of your work, then what you've planned will take place … Far better to be right and poor than to be wrong and rich. We plan the way we want to live, but only God makes us able to live it"* (16:1-3,6-9 MSG). It is worth recalling Proverbs is primarily about setting out the way of wisdom that we need to follow, and however smart we may consider ourselves to be, we can't outsmart the Almighty who knows our motives and can foresee the outcome of our actions. This is why we need to commit all that we do to God and doing it His way. Even if we have little to show for our efforts, what matters is to do it the way He decrees and for Him. If there is a moral here, it is better to be humble than proud, poor than rich.

Pride is associated with feelings of pleasure in achievement, accomplishment, of something we have done, or are, or in someone else, and is often associated with conceit, egotism, vanity, vainglory, and one's own appearance or status in life. It is a dangerous thing that can take us away from God. Besides today's text, we read *"A man's pride shall bring him low: but honour shall uphold the humble in spirit"* (29:23). We are warned: *"Love not the world, neither the things that are in the world. If any man love the world, the love of the Father is not in him. For all that is in the world, the lust of the flesh, and the lust of the eyes, and the pride of life, is not of the Father, but is of the world"* 1 John 2:15,16, and *"God resisteth the proud, but giveth grace unto the humble"* James 4:6. The Bible is full of examples of man's (and also Satan's) pride. While frustratingly the proud person may seem to prosper for a season, he will come to a sad end and will eventually fall, while the humble person will be exalted – eventually. Pride is a trap we can easily fall into, for such is the human heart. The truth is *"The heart is deceitful above all things, and desperately wicked: who can know it?"* Jeremiah 17:9.

Prayer: Lord we commit our being and doing to following the way of wisdom. Forgive our pride and deliver us from it. We thank you that you hate pride and love humility, honouring the humble. May we ever identify with the humble.

Day 17: The quiet life (17:1)

"Better is a dry morsel, and quietness therewith, than an house full of sacrifices with strife."

It would be dishonest to encapsulate the many profound and different thoughts in what we know are artificial demarcations, *i.e.* chapters of the Bible, under a single title, but one recurring theme of Ch.17 is the agreeableness of a quiet and peaceful life. Again, Solomon masterfully used powerful illustrations to make an important point. In our text, it is about how much better it is to eat a very simple diet and have a life of contented peace than one where one can eat rich food at banquets, but there is strife and aggravation. There is something to be said too for applying the maxim *"godliness with contentment is great gain"* (1Timothy 6:6). Peace (completeness, soundness, welfare) (Hebrew: *shalom*) is important to have and is to be highly regarded, occurring 237 times in the OT, and was how YHWH wanted to bless his people. It is seen in the blessing: *"The Lord bless thee, and keep thee ... and give thee peace"* Numbers 6:24-26. We do well to follow the counsel: *"Follow peace with all men, and holiness, without which no man shall see the Lord"* Hebrews 12:14. Also relevant is that the coming Messiah is called *"The Prince of Peace"* (Isaiah 9:6) and *"of the increase of his government and peace there shall be no end"* (Isaiah 9:7) and God *"wilt keep him in perfect peace, whose mind is stayed on thee: because he trusteth in thee"* (Isaiah 26:3). Also *"My son, forget not my law; but let thine heart keep my commandments: For length of days, and long life, and peace, shall they add to thee"* (3:2).

A further observation about the desirability of peace is our attitude, especially when wronged by others, by our not stirring up trouble when it is easy to do so and being a calming influence in situations when peace is needed and which complements Jesus' *"blessed are the peacemakers"* teaching: *"He that covereth a transgression seeketh love; but he that repeateth a matter separateth very friends ... The beginning of strife is as when one letteth out water: therefore leave off contention, before it be meddled with"* (17:9,14). One could also add *"A reproof entereth more into a wise man than an hundred stripes into a fool"* (17:10) and the sort of priorities a peaceful person has: *"Friends love through all kinds of weather, and families stick together in all kinds of trouble"* (17:17 MSG). The chapter ends with astute observations why a peaceful approach is important: *"He that hath knowledge spareth his words: and a man of understanding is of an excellent spirit. Even a fool, when he holdeth his peace, is counted wise: and he that shutteth his lips is esteemed a man of understanding"* (17:27,28).

Prayer: We thank you Lord: blessed are the peacemakers and thank you for them. Make me a channel of your peace; where there is hatred, let me bring your love.

Day 18: The way of the fool (18:2)

"A fool hath no delight in understanding, but that his heart may discover itself." Or *"Fools care nothing for thoughtful discourse; all they do is run off at the mouth"* (MSG).

It has been said the world can be divided into three camps: fools, villains and the good guys and all of us take in elements from each, in varying proportions. For Solomon, there are just two categories: the fools (that also included villains (or the wicked)) and the wise (*i.e.* the good guys). One major theme of Proverbs was to present the stark choice we all need to make between following the way of foolishness and that of wisdom, giving numerous, graphic examples of what each entails and the outcomes of our choices. Of the 189 references to "fool" in the Bible, 78 are found in the Book of Proverbs. Clearly, the way of wisdom is the one to be commended and it begins with the fear of the Lord. In today's text, we see one of many examples of how the fool acts and one no doubt we have observed and perhaps have been guilty of, setting out our own erroneous opinions and shutting out any challenge that we could be wrong.

Further texts, specifically citing the fool, his ways and his end are: "*A fool hath no delight in understanding, but that his heart may discover itself … A fool's lips enter into contention, and his mouth calleth for strokes. A fool's mouth is his destruction, and his lips are the snare of his soul*" (18:2,6-7). Another example is: "*The words of a talebearer are as wounds, and they go down into the innermost parts of the belly. He also that is slothful in his work is brother to him that is a great waster*" (18:8,9). Then we see foolish and wise behaviour and their consequences contrasted: "*Before destruction the heart of man is haughty, and before honour is humility. He that answereth a matter before he heareth it, it is folly and shame unto him*" (18:12,13). But wisdom always wins through: "*The name of the Lord is a strong tower: the righteous runneth into it, and is safe … The heart of the prudent getteth knowledge; and the ear of the wise seeketh knowledge*" (18:10,15). After laying down the challenge of following the way of wisdom, we end our thought for today with some NT wisdom as to how me might now proceed: "*If you don't know what you're doing, pray to the Father. He loves to help. You'll get his help, and won't be condescended to when you ask for it. Ask boldly, believingly, without a second thought. People who "worry their prayers" are like wind-whipped waves. Don't think you're going to get anything from the Master that way, adrift at sea, keeping all your options open*" (James 1:5-8 MSG).

Prayer: Dear Lord and Father of mankind, forgive our foolish ways. Thank you that the way of the wise and the way of the fool have been so clearly set out in your Word. May we choose the way of wisdom and look to you and your Word.

Day 19: Concerning the poor (19:1)

"Better is the poor that walketh in his integrity, than he that is perverse in his lips, and is a fool."

Today's chapter again has lots of good stuff we are not even going to look at. But there is an important theme here that is referred to elsewhere in Proverbs – that of dealing with the poor and what to make out of poverty. While poverty is not something most of us would long for, unless taking the vow of poverty (and chastity and obedience, also relevant to how we might wish to live), Solomon, who ironically was very rich, could see the value of being poor as the price to pay for keeping one's integrity, having noted how riches (not wrong in itself) could lead one off the straight path, especially if it is a result of bribes or ill-gotten gain. He states the obvious: people don't want to have anything to do with those who are poor (how true that is still), even if entreated by them, but will chase after the rich: *"Wealth maketh many friends; but the poor is separated from his neighbour … All the brethren of the poor do hate him: how much more do his friends go far from him? he pursueth them with words, yet they are wanting to him"* (19:4,7). There is a popular song titled "**Money can't buy me love**" and, who knows, the Beatles could have got their inspiration from Solomon: *"House and riches are the inheritance of fathers: and a prudent wife is from the Lord"* (19:14). As for how we should respond, the answer is clear and it comes with a reward worth having: *"He that hath pity upon the poor lendeth unto the Lord; and that which he hath given will he pay him again"* (19:17). As for us, our text is reiterated: *"The desire of a man is his kindness: and a poor man is better than a liar"* (19:22).

Proverbs has a lot more to say about the poor and poverty but, in rounding off today's thought, we jump to the end, on what appears to be a sensible balance between riches and poverty: *"Remove far from me vanity and lies: give me neither poverty nor riches; feed me with food convenient for me: Lest I be full, and deny thee, and say, Who is the Lord? or lest I be poor, and steal, and take the name of my God in vain"* (30:8,9). Then a final exhortation: *"Open thy mouth, judge righteously, and plead the cause of the poor and needy"* (31:9). We end quoting Jesus at the start of His ministry, himself quoting Isaiah: *"The Spirit of the Lord is upon me, because he hath anointed me to preach the gospel to the poor; he hath sent me to heal the broken hearted, to preach deliverance to the captives, and recovering of sight to the blind, to set at liberty them that are bruised"* Luke 4:18 and *"Blessed be ye poor: for yours is the kingdom of God"* Luke 6:20.

Prayer: May we never despise the poor. Thank you, Lord, you love to bless the poor. Thank you Jesus when you lived here on earth you identified with the poor. May we be content with our lot, recognising integrity is what matters more.

Day 20: The pure in heart (20:9)

"Who can say, I have made my heart clean, I am pure from my sin?"

For someone who follows the Lord, a verse like this can hit us like bolts out of the blue. The natural tendency is take the moral high ground, even if wrong. After all, a person may fear the Lord and seek righteousness with an aim for his actions to be only that which is pure. Yet our text does not qualify "who" is referred to, so we can take it personally and face up to the reality that even with our most noble and doing it for the glory of God and the good of others motives, there is always the possibility of an element of impurity creeping in, and if nothing else it should keep us humble and take us off our "holy" high horse when challenged. Looking at the context (verse before and verse after), we read *"Leaders who know their business and care keep a sharp eye out for the shoddy and cheap, or who among us can be trusted to be always diligent and honest? Switching price tags and padding the expense account are two things God hates"* (20:8-10 MSG). Both the before and after the act verses refer to what purity looks like in real terms: in our business dealings we must give of our best and be honest in all that we do.

Related texts on this theme to be found in our chapter include: *"Most men will proclaim every one his own goodness: but a faithful man who can find?"* (20:6), and how true it is, suggesting our focus should be on being loyal and loving rather than merely talking about it. Then we are told a sober truth of how one is known by what one does, and while it is to do with children it could well apply to anyone of us: *"Even a child is known by his doings, whether his work be pure, and whether it be right"* (20:11). Finally, an even more sober truth is how God is in charge of human life, and watches and examines us inside and out: *"The spirit of man is the candle of the Lord, searching all the inward parts of the belly"* (20:27).

But we wrap up our thoughts on the importance of purity with this quote from the OT: *"Who shall ascend into the hill of the Lord? or who shall stand in his holy place? He that hath clean hands, and a pure heart; who hath not lifted up his soul unto vanity, nor sworn deceitfully* (Psalm 24:3,4), followed by one from the NT, part of Jesus' teachings, part of the beatitudes: *"Blessed are the pure in heart: for they shall see God"* Matthew 5:8. In both our verses we are told that the reward of a pure heart is we shall see God, and that ought to be our aim.

Prayer: Search me, O God, and know my heart: try me, and know my thoughts: And see if there be any wicked way in me, and lead me in the way everlasting. We thank you Lord that all your ways are pure. Cleanse us from all impurity, even if the refining process is to be a painful one, so that our hearts may be pure.

Day 21: A good leader (21:1)

"The king's heart is in the hand of the Lord, as the rivers of water: he turneth it whithersoever he will."

The first thing to say is today's text is not about good leaders *per se*. It is about kings, which in OT times were rulers of empires, nations and sometimes cities. Moreover, any king, the bad as well as the good. Proverbs has a lot to say about kings. While not using terms like "leader", it does talk about leadership qualities, typically associated with the wise. In today's chapter, the notion of the heart is further developed: *"Every way of a man is right in his own eyes: but the Lord pondereth the hearts"* (21:2) and something to expect from kings: *"To do justice and judgment is more acceptable to the Lord than sacrifice"* (21:3). And to complement: *"By me (wisdom) kings reign, and princes decree justice"* (8:15).

Today's meditation was written on the day the USA inaugurated its 46th President. Few would dispute there are wide differences between POTUS 45 and 46 and many will have strong views on their relative merits. What is relevant as far as today's text goes, made here more explicit, is: *"Good leadership is a channel of water controlled by God; he directs it to whatever ends he chooses"* (MSG). It seems an incredible and unlikely notion that God controls the hearts of kings, directing them in the way he will, especially when the history of the world is littered with examples of bad kings who inflicted untold evil on their subjects. Our experience in the world of politics and business is that the poor candidate may get promoted to positions of power and the good often gets left behind. Ours is not to dispute God, but pray: *"I exhort therefore, that, first of all, supplications, prayers, intercessions, and giving of thanks, be made for all men; For kings, and for all that are in authority; that we may lead a quiet and peaceable life in all godliness and honesty"* (1 Timothy 2:1,2).

Righteous and godly are not the words that spring to mind when we think of Nebuchadnezzar (Daniel 4), Cyrus (Isaiah 45), Jehu (2 Kings 9), but these were influential kings whose hearts were clearly in the hands of the Lord. These accomplished many of His purposes, regardless. While on the subject of good leaders, what about us? Maybe the circumstances of life may put us firmly in "the led" camp. Yet we can lead by example, following the way of wisdom and be blessed: *"The king's favour is toward a wise servant"* (14:35), *"Righteous lips are the delight of kings"* (16:13), *"He that loveth pureness of heart, for the grace of his lips the king shall be his friend"* (22:11), *"Seest thou a man diligent in his business? he shall stand before kings"* (22:29).

Prayer: We pray for kings and those in authority Lord. We thank you the king's heart is in your hand. Whatever our station in life, may we be good and wise.

Day 22: A good name (22:1)

"A good name is rather to be chosen than great riches, and loving favour rather than silver and gold."

We come to the end of Solomon's own wise sayings and from 22:17 onwards we find him putting together a compendium of sayings of the wise. Our text today is about the importance of a good name, more important than lots of possessions etc. While some may care little for a good reputation, for Solomon this matters and we can all think of the tragedy that ensues when a person loses his good name. Our text ties in with "*Let not mercy and truth forsake thee: bind them about thy neck; write them upon the table of thine heart: So shalt thou find favour and good understanding in the sight of God and man*" (3:3,4) and "*Blessings are upon the head of the just: but violence covereth the mouth of the wicked. The memory of the just is blessed: but the name of the wicked shall rot*" (10:6,7). Both take the view that earning a reputation for living the good life, while alive and when dead, matters more than anything else. Tying in with the theme of a good name and what truly matters is: "*By humility and the fear of the Lord are riches, and honour, and life*" (22:4). Regarding the ending of this section, a friend once wisely wrote: "*The king, the wicked, the mocker, the wise, the proud, the diligent, the sluggard, the false witness, the guilty, the innocent, the rich, the poor, the prudent, the generous, the wife, the adulteress and the child all come on stage for a final curtain-call! And so does 'The Righteous One' 'The Lord' and 'The Maker.'*"

We begin our section, which covers further wise sayings, on a confident and entreating note: "*Bow down thine ear, and hear the words of the wise, and apply thine heart unto my knowledge … That thy trust may be in the Lord*" (22:17,19). We see again how important truth is: "*Have not I written to thee excellent things in counsels and knowledge, That I might make thee know the certainty of the words of truth; that thou mightest answer the words of truth to them that send unto thee?*" (22:20,21) We are reminded again of our obligations to the less well off: "*Rob not the poor, because he is poor: neither oppress the afflicted in the gate: For the Lord will plead their cause*" (22:22,23). We are warned: "*Make no friendship with an angry man; and with a furious man*" (22:24). We are reminded of the need for wisdom in our dealings: "*Be not thou one of them that strike hands, or of them that are sureties for debts*" (22:26) and how to treat others: "*Remove not the ancient landmark, which thy fathers have set*" (22:28).

Prayer: We thank you Lord for the wisdom of Solomon and the wise. May we not lose our good name through folly, even if we do lose our possessions. May we put doing the right thing at the top of our list, who love truth and our neighbour.

Day 23: Buy the truth (23:23)

"Buy the truth, and sell it not; also wisdom, instruction, and understanding."

These sayings of the wise do well to complement those of Solomon. We have a warning against gluttony, especially if in influential company (23:1-3). We are told not to waste our energies in getting rich (23:4-5). We need to beware of the tight-fisted person (23:6-8). We are told not to waste our time engaging with fools (23:9) We must not stealthily move back the boundary lines or cheat orphans out of their property (23:10-11) tying in with one idea behind *"Remove not the ancient landmark"* (22:28), and that of preserving the godly heritage passed down through the generations. We must give ourselves to disciplined instruction (23:12), not to be afraid of correcting our children (including if needed the use of corporal punishment) – for a wise child will make one happy parent (23:13-16). We are not to envy *"sinners"* but rather to fear God (23:17-18) (a thought we will return to tomorrow). We are (or at least "my son" is) told again to avoid loose women (23:26-28). Then there is some graphically illustrated counsel on why we must not drink too much wine and get drunk (23:19-21) and (23:29-35).

Which leads us to our text for today *"Buy truth – don't sell it for love or money; buy wisdom, buy education, buy insight"* (23:23 MSG). The follow-on to this is also relevant given that the writer is keen to pass this on to his children and as a thought for those who are parents this should be our priority too: *"The father of the righteous shall greatly rejoice: and he that begetteth a wise child shall have joy of him. Thy father and thy mother shall be glad, and she that bare thee shall rejoice"* (23:24,25). Truth is up there with wisdom and righteousness in terms of importance as far as Proverbs is concerned and, interestingly, is linked three times with mercy, reminding us there is a balance to be had and of the one who was full of grace and truth (John 1:14). We noted in the previous chapter the importance attached to truth: *"That I might make thee know the certainty of the words of truth; that thou mightest answer the words of truth to them that send unto thee?"* (22:21) Earlier on in Proverbs we were told: *"Let not mercy and truth forsake thee: bind them about thy neck; write them upon the table of thine heart"* (3:3). While wanting to keep with the non-moralising tone of Proverbs, we do well to take up the challenge to seek out and be exemplars of truth in all aspects of our lives, making it our priority in everything we do and following Him who is the Truth.

Prayer: We are so grateful Jesus you are the Truth, are full of truth and you told us that the Truth will set us free. May we seek after and live out truth, whatever the cost, and in a world full of falsehood and deception, help us to discern what is true and stand with those who seek and sometimes suffer because of the truth.

Day 24: Do not envy evil men (24:1)

"Be not thou envious against evil men, neither desire to be with them."

We can link today's text nicely with what we read yesterday: "*Let not thine heart envy sinners: but be thou in the fear of the Lord all the day long. For surely there is an end; and thine expectation shall not be cut off*" (23:17). Continuing therefore, we find our wise man giving good reasons for not envying the bad man, for all his pretentions, plausibility and ability to gain a following: "*for their heart studieth destruction, and their lips talk of mischief*" (24:2). He focuses our attention onto what truly matters – concerning how we need to build in our lives: "*Through wisdom is an house builded; and by understanding it is established*" (24:3). He then goes on to talk about the virtues of the wise and the rewards of the way of wisdom, comparing it with a critique of the way of the fool and the destructive end of foolishness. "*For a just man falleth seven times, and riseth up again: but the wicked shall fall into mischief*" (24:16). And just in case we miss the punch of today's text, the points are further reinforced: "*Fret not thyself because of evil men, neither be thou envious at the wicked: For there shall be no reward to the evil man; the candle of the wicked shall be put out*" (24:19,20).

Today's text ties in with an often repeated theme of the Psalmist, which at the start declares: "*Blessed is the man that walketh not in the counsel of the ungodly, nor standeth in the way of sinners, nor sitteth in the seat of the scornful*" Psalm 1:1. It seems the Psalmist, often David before he became king, was obsessed with the wicked; not only because of their attacks on the righteous but they seemed to get away with it, for example: "*Fret not thyself because of evildoers, neither be thou envious against the workers of iniquity. For they shall soon be cut down like the grass, and wither as the green herb. Trust in the Lord, and do good; so shalt thou dwell in the land, and verily thou shalt be fed. Delight thyself also in the Lord: and he shall give thee the desires of thine heart. Commit thy way unto the Lord; trust also in him; and he shall bring it to pass*" (37:1-5). The writer of the Psalms, like Proverbs, was well aware that the bad people attracted foolish people who flocked to their side, often because they did thrive, at least for a season. The reality is that today the bad person is just as, if not more, likely to hold a position of influence and esteem than the good person, and even seem to thrive. But the wise take a long-term view knowing, whatever the price they have to pay, walking in the way of wisdom is far better than even touching the way of the wicked.

Prayer: We are sorry Lord for the times we have envied and fretted ourselves over evil men. May we stand with the poor and righteous because we know that is where your heart is. We thank you, when the just man falls, he is able to get up.

Day 25: Be kind to your enemies (25:21,22)

"If thine enemy be hungry, give him bread to eat; and if he be thirsty, give him water to drink: For thou shalt heap coals of fire upon his head, and the Lord shall reward thee."

We are back with Solomon's wisdom, but here is what was compiled under King Hezekiah, some 250 years later. Hezekiah was a standout good king, no doubt influenced by Solomon's wisdom. As always, we find in this chapter lots of good stuff, some of which we can look at only briefly before attending to our text for today. We begin by revisiting kings whose significance we see once again is important: *"It is the glory of God to conceal a thing: but the honour of kings is to search out a matter. The heaven for height, and the earth for depth, and the heart of kings is unsearchable"* (25:2,3) and *"Take away the wicked from before the king, and his throne shall be established in righteousness. Put not forth thyself in the presence of the king, and stand not in the place of great men"* (25:5,6).

There is wisdom concerning dealing with our neighbours: *"Go not forth hastily to strive, lest thou know not what to do in the end thereof, when thy neighbour hath put thee to shame. Debate thy cause with thy neighbour himself; and discover not a secret to another"* (25:8,9). There are timeless truths: *"Withdraw thy foot from thy neighbour's house; lest he be weary of thee, and so hate thee"* (25:17) and truths that always resonate: *"As cold waters to a thirsty soul, so is good news from a far country"* (25:25). Then there are truths so profound because they are about what we may have observed: *"A righteous man falling down before the wicked is as a troubled fountain, and a corrupt spring"* (25:26). And more! Being kind to our enemies is a theme that is picked up in the NT: *"Recompense to no man evil for evil. Provide things honest in the sight of all men. If it be possible, as much as lieth in you, live peaceably with all men. Dearly beloved, avenge not yourselves, but rather give place unto wrath: for it is written, Vengeance is mine; I will repay, saith the Lord. Therefore if thine enemy hunger, feed him; if he thirst, give him drink: for in so doing thou shalt heap coals of fire on his head. Be not overcome of evil, but overcome evil with good"* Romans 12:17-21. There is much to challenge us with this teaching – while we can point to some or other scripture telling us that bad people will get their comeuppance, that is something for God to sort out, for there is a better way! Our kind response to an unkind action by someone who wrongs us, who upsets us, could well lead him to repentance.

Prayer: We thank you for the example of our Lord Jesus Christ who forgave his enemies and taught us to love our enemies and pray for those who persecute us. Help us dear Lord to be kind to others, including those who have wronged us.

Day 26: Dealing with fools (26:4)

"Answer not a fool according to his folly, lest thou also be like unto him."

While today's chapter brings out an assortment of important thoughts, there is an underlying theme – it is to do with the way of the fool and how to respond to him. The ideal response is encapsulated in today's verse: *"Don't respond to the stupidity of a fool; you'll only look foolish yourself"* (MSG) and maybe to avoid him altogether. *"Answer a fool according to his folly, lest he be wise in his own conceit"* (26:5) and if we do answer a fool it needs to be in simple terms so he doesn't get conceited (26:6). We live in a world where folly abounds, maybe subtly. It is inevitable that ours and the path of fools cross, so we need to know what to do. We need to be on our look out to identify what that amounts to and, if we have to respond, find the best way to go about it. Our text provides the sort of advice we ought to have taken in the past and instead we answered a fool according to his folly, when the best approach was not to take the bait.

The chapter begins by reflecting how inappropriate it is to honour a fool (26:1) and also (26:8) – although sadly we live in a world where that happens all too often. As far as Solomon is concerned, a fool recycles silliness and cannot be trusted. For the rest of this chapter, he goes through different sorts of people, all of which we might place in the fool category. There are those who loaf around, finding excuses for their inaction (26:13-15). There are dreamers who fantasize their self-importance; who think they are smarter than anyone else (26:16). There are those who interfere in other peoples' quarrels (26:17). There are those who are party to deception, shrugging it off as if it were nothing (26:18-19). There is the argumentative sort that invariably adds fuel to the fire (26:21). There are the listeners to and the spreaders of gossip, and we know how much damage all that causes (26:20,22). There are those who smooth talk and appear friendly but behind the façade there is the intent to do people down (26:23-26). Then there are the malicious, whose malice invariably backfires (26:27), liars who hate their victims (26:28) and the flatterers who sabotage trust (26:28). Lessons we might learn from these observations could include that in this wonderful world in which we live there are those who would taint its wonder; folly can manifest itself in many sorts of ways; we need to beware of fools on our own doorstep; we must not be like them and, as well, accept the harsh reality that *"the great God that formed all things both rewardeth the fool, and rewardeth transgressors"* (26:10).

Prayer: As we go about our day-to-day business Lord, help us to avoid the way of the fool and deal with every instance of folly we find in the way that is best. Thank you for your word that teaches us the way the wise need to follow.

Day 27: Not boasting of tomorrow (27:1)

"Boast not thyself of tomorrow; for thou knowest not what a day may bring forth."

Today's chapter contains many wonderful blessed thoughts. We first consider our text, reinforcing: *"A man's heart deviseth his way: but the Lord directeth his steps"* (16:9). Most of us are guilty of boasting about tomorrow before it happens, thinking we have everything figured out and that things will turn out just as we hoped. As far as Solomon was concerned, that is foolishness, for we cannot predict what is going to happen and likely we have all found what happens is often not what we expected. The right approach is to live each moment for God. This is brought home in Jesus' parable of a man who knocks down his barns to build bigger ones so eventually he can take it easy. He ends: *"But God said unto him, thou fool, this night thy soul shall be required of thee: then whose shall those things be, which thou hast provided? So is he that layeth up treasure for himself, and is not rich toward God"* Luke 12:16-21.

Our second text is: *"Faithful are the wounds of a friend; but the kisses of an enemy are deceitful"* (27:6), preceded by: *"Open rebuke is better than secret love"* (27:5). Friends who look out for us are precious, especially if their concern is such that they will tell us where we are going wrong if that is what we are doing. We ought to be thankful for that even if our initial response is to feel affronted. In contrast, there are those who flatter us, even when we are doing wrong; such actions are deceitful, and continuing along such a path unchecked will no doubt prove ruinous. We need to be the sort of friend that tells it as it is (caution: there are ways to do this and ways *not* to) and to prize friends who rebuke us.

Our third text is: *"Iron sharpeneth iron; so a man sharpeneth the countenance of his friend"* (27:17). If we are going to be useful and effective in life and in God's service, we need to be sharp and ready to respond, so we can handle whatever life throws up in the best possible way. There are ways to help achieve this, such as reading the Bible and prayer, but another way is being encouraged by another person, and often this is something we can reciprocate. How often can we look back in gratitude when someone has spoken a timely word or done something that has somehow invigorated us when we needed it most. Just as earlier with the friend who puts us straight, even if it is wounding us, so we also can appreciate the friend who sharpens us toward greatness, and we can be that friend to others.

Prayer: We thank you Lord you hold the keys to all unknown. May we never take for granted what we have or presume for the future. May we be a faithful friend who will say things as they really are and be an encourager to other people.

Day 28: Righteous and wicked compared (28:1)

"The wicked flee when no man pursueth: but the righteous are bold as a lion."

Just as Proverbs often contrasts the wise with the foolish, it also does so with the righteous and the wicked. "Righteous" appears 75 times in Proverbs, four times in this chapter. "Wicked" appears 95 times in Proverbs, five times in this chapter. Three times, including today's text, the righteous are compared with the wicked, and it is quite clear which camp we ought to be in. In another rendering of today's text, we read: "*The wicked are edgy with guilt, ready to run off even when no one's after them; Honest people are relaxed and confident, bold as lions*" MSG). Whatever it is bugging the wicked, he is on edge, ready to flee at the slightest provocation, even at false alarms. This is in marked contrast to the righteous, who can confidently and serenely stand his ground whatever it is he is faced with. Seen in such a light it is clearly evident which camp we are going to be better off in.

Our second comparison is: "*When righteous men do rejoice, there is great glory: but when the wicked rise, a man is hidden*" (28:12) or "*When good people are promoted, everything is great, but when the bad are in charge, watch out!*" (MSG). What is being observed is a simple fact and one we would have seen, maybe many times. Too often the baddies get to the top and the goodies are left behind, and the result is misery. The opposite is true when good people are promoted and bad people demoted. In God's kingdom that will be the case.

Our third comparison is: "*When the wicked rise, men hide themselves: but when they perish, the righteous increase*" (28:28) or "*When corruption takes over, good people go underground, but when the crooks are thrown out, it's safe to come out*" (MSG). Corruption in government is horribly evident and something we ought to avoid and counter. If corruption is rooted out; people can breathe easy. In line with his non-moralising tone, Solomon doesn't follow up by calling for a righteous crusade to promote good people and root out corruption, possibly realising for most of us our power to do so is limited. But we can be those who feature among the righteous, who the Lord will honour. It is clear the people we should be: "*He that is of a proud heart stirreth up strife: but he that putteth his trust in the Lord shall be made fat. He that trusteth in his own heart is a fool: but whoso walketh wisely, he shall be delivered. He that giveth unto the poor shall not lack: but he that hideth his eyes shall have many a curse*" (28:25-27).

Prayer: We grieve when wickedness prevails, but thank you Lord the wicked and the righteous receive their just desserts. We pray for righteous government and for corruption to be rooted out. Help us to follow the path of righteousness.

Day 29: The fear of man (29:25)

"The fear of man bringeth a snare: but whoso putteth his trust in the Lord shall be safe."

As we approach the end of Proverbs and before handing over to the two "guest" wise men, we round off the sayings of Solomon with lots of timely repetition. Today we will do a quick recap before ending with our thought for the day. We begin with the recurring theme of reproof and discipline. Firstly, as applying to us personally: *"He, that being often reproved hardeneth his neck, shall suddenly be destroyed, and that without remedy"* (29:1). Secondly, about the bringing up of children (today's parents take note since the sad result of ignoring such counsel is all too evident): *"The rod and reproof give wisdom: but a child left to himself bringeth his mother to shame … Correct thy son, and he shall give thee rest; yea, he shall give delight unto thy soul"* (29:15,17). We consider kings and rulers, reminding us again why we want them to be good and wise: *"When the righteous are in authority, the people rejoice: but when the wicked beareth rule, the people mourn … The king by judgment establisheth the land: but he that receiveth gifts overthroweth it … If a ruler hearken to lies, all his servants are wicked … The king that faithfully judgeth the poor, his throne shall be established for ever"* (29:2,4,12,14). There is still more we can find in our chapter on themes covered earlier, notably contrasts: the wise and the foolish, the righteous and the wicked, the angry and the peace loving, and the humble and the proud.

But before our text for today, another often quoted text is: *"Where there is no vision, the people perish: but he that keepeth the law, happy is he"* (29:18). Wouldn't it be lovely to see a new generation with the sort of vision to respond to: *"If people can't see what God is doing, they stumble all over themselves; But when they attend to what he reveals, they are most blessed"* (MSG). Yet we can be people with God's vision. So back to our text for today: *"The fear of human opinion disables; trusting in God protects you from that"* (MSG). Tragically, history and experience are littered with examples of people who have missed God's best because they fear what others might think and have gone with the flow that is not what God intended. Thank God too for those who did what our text suggests and, as they trusted in God to protect them, they entered into the flow of God's stream. The challenge before us is to partner with God by being party to the vision He wants us to have and not being deterred because of the fear of man.

Prayer: Lord, we are continually amazed by the precious truths that leap out of your Word. Help us be those who keep your law and own the vision you have for the peoples of the earth. We are sorry when we succumb to the fear of man and rather may we put our trust in you, knowing we are safe and your way is best.

Day 30: God's pure word (30:5)

"Every word of God is pure: he is a shield unto them that put their trust in him."

Today's chapter are *"the words of Agur the son of Jakeh"* about whom we know little other than what his words reveal about him. He appeared to be very humble (content with the peaceful life, away from the limelight, and having just enough to get by) and wise (given his insights into many things that are humanity and nature related that most miss). He begins by recognising how little he or anyone else knows about God: *"I neither learned wisdom, nor have the knowledge of the holy"* (30:3). In today's text, he makes an apt observation about God's word that we do well to heed. It is pure (unlike so much else we come across), and throws in a related thought of God being a shield, *i.e.* a protector to those who trust in Him. He follows this up with the thought we must not add to God's word and adulterate it: *"Add thou not unto his words, lest he reprove thee, and thou be found a liar"* (30:6). In making his observation concerning purity, he reinforces what we learn in the Psalms: *"The statutes of the Lord are right, rejoicing the heart: the commandment of the Lord is pure, enlightening the eyes"* Psalm 19:8 and *"Thy word is very pure: therefore thy servant loveth it"* Psalm 119:140. Just as Proverbs encourages wisdom over foolishness etc., so it does purity over impurity.

Going back to his contentment, he prays for two things in life: *"Remove far from me vanity and lies: give me neither poverty nor riches; feed me with food convenient for me: Lest I be full, and deny thee, and say, Who is the Lord? or lest I be poor, and steal, and take the name of my God in vain"* (30:8,9). While we do not expect folk to pray quite along these lines, we do well to take note. As for Agur's words that follow, as one commentator remarked: "He begins with a frank observation of human wickedness (30:10-15a). Then his unique way of making vivid comparisons has seven main focuses: the pain of childlessness (30:15b-16), the disrespecting of parents (30:17), the mystery of romantic relationships (30:18-19), the shamelessness of adultery (30:20), the agony of an unloved wife (30:21-23), the various kinds of wisdom (30:24-28), and the slightly comical nature of human power! (30:29-31)". He ends just as he had begun, on a note of wise humility, and one we would do well to follow: *"If thou hast done foolishly in lifting up thyself, or if thou hast thought evil, lay thine hand upon thy mouth. Surely the churning of milk bringeth forth butter, and the wringing of the nose bringeth forth blood: so the forcing of wrath bringeth forth strife"* (30:32,33).

Prayer: Lord, we thank you every word you give is pure and you are a shield to those who trust in you. We thank you for people like Agur, who show humble contentment, and are able to discern your wisdom. May we too do likewise.

Day 31: A God-fearing woman (31:30)

"Favour is deceitful, and beauty is vain: but a woman that feareth the Lord, she shall be praised."

Today we come to our second guest contributor and it is appropriate in a book written by a father for his son and aimed at men, that the ladies have the last word, and they do so in more ways than one. As with Agur, we know little of today's author, Lemuel, other than he was a king who had been taught well by his mother, evidenced by his words. He goes over ground already well covered – stay away from wanton women and don't get drunk, and then makes a profound point that will no doubt please those who major on social justice: *"Open thy mouth for the dumb in the cause of all such as are appointed to destruction. Open thy mouth, judge righteously, and plead the cause of the poor and needy"* (31:8,9). We have noted already that the key virtue of Proverbs – wisdom – is a lady. Along with the importance of the father's teaching, on an equal footing is that of the mother.

But Proverbs ends (31:10-31) with reflecting on the subject of a wife of noble character. It does so by way of an acrostic poem (each line starting with the next letter in the Hebrew alphabet) espousing some of the virtues discussed in earlier chapters. It attempts to answer the question, and at least suggests it is one that any man looking for his partner in life ought to be asking: *"Who can find a virtuous woman?"* (31:10a) and then gives plenty of back-up as to why he considers *"her price is far above rubies"* (31:10b). While we may wryly smile at the thought of this woman, who gets up early to organise the household servants, and reflect he lived on a different planet to the one we are used to, yet we have to agree she is pretty awesome and if those of us (who are unmarried men) find such a ruby, then we are blessed indeed. She is a hard worker and an astute, honest businesswoman. She is a good employer, gives generously to the poor, provides well for her household. Her husband has full confidence in her, her husband is respected at the "city gate" and her children arise and call her blessed (31:11,23,28). She is clothed with strength and dignity; she can laugh at the days to come; she speaks with wisdom, and gives faithful instruction (31:25-26).

So, Proverbs comes to an end, singing her praises and commending her virtues that far excel the mere outward show we too often see: *"Many women have done wonderful things, but you've outclassed them all! Charm can mislead and beauty soon fades. The woman to be admired and praised is the woman who lives in the Fear-of-God. Give her everything she deserves! Adorn her life with praises!"* (31:29-31 MSG).

Prayer: We thank you Lord for the many wonderful lessons we have learned in Proverbs. We thank you for the noble woman whose price is far above rubies.

Proving Proverbs

Regardless of the number of times we read or refer to a particular Bible passage, something fresh or new is likely to jump out of the page, and this has been my experience throughout the period I have been preparing these 31 meditations in Proverbs. It often meant reading in two or more versions and then doing cross reference checks in order to get the right meaning and context, followed by a good deal of meditating – just as applicable with Proverbs as with the Song of Songs. Despite trying to be clever by attempting to cover all of Proverbs main points, having given myself 31 bites of the cherry, I have no doubt I have failed and the challenge for readers is to find things I missed. As for discovering things afresh, as far as Proverbs went, it was my daily experience, despite thinking I knew the book well, and then finding I did not. Then there was the experience of being tested on some point I had reflected on a little earlier, and finding sometimes I failed. Another beautifully odd experience was reading the chapter for the day in our family prayer times and finding something amazing, earlier missed. Yet another is discovering how wide and often Proverbs is quoted in every day usage.

I would definitely recommend it if one were to include Proverbs in one's daily Bible reading routine, perhaps concentrating on one thought each day and doing so along with Psalms and the rest of the Bible. Irrespective of how many times one was to go round the block so to speak, there is likely something new to be found each time. Some of the great themes of life that ought to be of interest to an earnest follower of YHWH are discussed in Proverbs: fear of the Lord, truth, wisdom, humility, purity, knowledge, understanding, righteousness, discipline, industry etc. Such qualities are well worth having and, while it is no guarantee that life will run as smoothly as we might hope, as our study of the next wisdom book, Ecclesiastes, will show, we will be better off having these qualities, than not having them, and following the way of wisdom is far better than the way of foolishness that will ever want to draw us away, along with its disastrous effects.

There is a refreshing down to earthiness about Proverbs, and an absence of religious mumbo jumbo and pretention. It was the writer's intention for readers to find true wisdom. While he had his own son in mind, whoever we are and whatever our station in life, if we are serious about following the Lord, we need wisdom and to discover what truly matters in life, by following its teachings. Given Proverbs is a practical rather than airy-fairy book, and covers real issues, we can identify what is written with today. Taking heed of what is taught will put us in good stead in facing the challenges of life, in both the big and little things. The challenge for us, the readers, is to prove these Proverbs for ourselves.

I alluded earlier to the idea of reading at least one proverb every day along with a Psalm (or part of when the Psalm is long) together with a plan to cover all of the rest of the Bible in a year. Having come out of meditating on the Proverbs, I am even more convinced that including this in one's daily Bible reading routine is a good idea if we believe gaining wisdom ought to be a priority. There is also the humbling realisation, I do not always apply what I know and that I know less than I thought I did. I say this in the light of reading or listening to people even recently discussing a pertinent, practical application to some or other verse from Proverbs that had struck them that had not previously occurred to me. All I can do is praise my all-wise God and be reminded of the words of the prophet: *"He hath shewed thee, O man, what is good; and what doth the Lord require of thee, but to do justly, and to love mercy, and to walk humbly with thy God?"* Micah 6:8.

Book 3

Ecclesiastes

Life under the sun

Introducing Ecclesiastes

Much of what I wanted to say generally on the Book of Ecclesiastes, the third book in this trilogy of Song of Songs, Proverbs and Ecclesiastes, has already been said in the *General Introduction* and in the first two books. The approach adopted will be similar, with a focus on providing thirty-one meditations, based on a single, and sometimes more than one, verse from the KJV version (allowing for the possibility other versions might give us a bigger wow factor and often provide fresh insights into the original text the KJV lacks), one page for each day of the month. Some verses from Ecclesiastes are fairly well known, just like Proverbs, yet this book is often not taught within church contexts, and its important message is not as well understood as it ought to be, which is a shame.

Ecclesiastes should be seen as a book for all ages – for the older generation making sense out of this world and having learned from the school of hard knocks what it says makes sense; for the younger, as a sober warning of what is to come and why they should *"remember now thy Creator in the days of thy youth"*, as well as the in-betweeners, being a useful foil to Proverbs with its hopeful message of the way of wisdom, and to Song of Songs with its recurring theme of love that conquers all. The main thrust of Ecclesiastes is the meaninglessness of *"life under the sun"*, ideally complementing that of the importance of following the way of wisdom (Proverbs) and the all-triumphant power of love (Song of Songs).

Regarding authorship, we are told right at the outset of the Book of Ecclesiastes that what is to follow are *"the words of the Preacher, the son of David, king in Jerusalem"* (1:1), although nowhere is the "Preacher" (also translated as Teacher) named. The word "Preacher" (Hebrew: *qoheleth*) occurs seven times in this book (and nowhere else in the Bible) and means (according to Strong) *"a collector of sentences"* and can also be taken to mean: *"one who addresses an assembly"*. The Latin title of this Book called Ecclesiastes, means *"speaker before an assembly"*.

While there is the possibility the author was another son of David, or even a later descendant, as far as this book is concerned, we will work on the basis the author is Solomon, if for no other reason than it ties in with my title and is what is traditionally believed. Many of the things that the Preacher claimed to have done during his life we know Solomon did or at least would have been ideally placed to do, and this is seen as he uses the rest of the book to elaborate on his opening salvo: *"Vanity of vanities, saith the Preacher, vanity of vanities; all is vanity. What profit hath a man of all his labour which he taketh under the sun?"* (1:2,3).

The notions of vanity (or pointlessness), referred to 29 times in Ecclesiastes, and of life under the sun, 31 times, is indicative of the author's central themes. Vanity (Hebrew: *hebel* – vapor, breath) well sums up what life under the sun is like. It is the realisation that this is how it is that helps us to make sense of life.

As for being in a position to wisely comment on what we know Solomon had seen and experienced, that too fits with the description of all the Preacher had done. "*Solomon loved the Lord, walking in the statutes of David his father*" (1 Kings 3:3). One night, the Lord appeared to Solomon and said, "*Ask what I shall give you*" (verse 5). In response, Solomon answered, "*Give your servant therefore an understanding mind to govern your people, that I may discern between good and evil, for who is able to govern this your great people?*" (verse 9). God also said "*I give you also what you have not asked, both riches and honour, so that no other king shall compare with you, all your days*" (1 Kings 3:13).

No doubt the position he found himself in (having time, power, wealth etc.) as well as wisdom from above, gave him ample opportunity to reflect as he did. One can't help wondering, though, why this same person, who began his reign so well, with every good intention, ended it so badly, by not practising what he preached. One of the good things to come out of his falling away toward the end is that Solomon better understood the consequences of where such actions might lead.

Reading through Ecclesiastes leaves us in little doubt the author had lived a long and full life, experiencing for himself and seeing it in others – highs and lows, triumphs and disasters, joy and sorrow, justice and injustice; from the very good to the very bad etc., suggesting by the time he got to write he was getting old. Just as Song of Songs reveals a young man's perspective (the way of love) and Proverbs that of a middle-aged man (the way of wisdom), reading Ecclesiastes leaves one with the impression that here was someone who had experienced many aspects of life but now he could no longer summon up much enthusiasm, being unimpressed, having seen it all, along with a sense of world weariness. If we are to come up with a third way, Ecclesiastes could be the way of "*life under the sun*".

Breaking down Proverbs (and even Song of Songs) into meaningful sections is easy compared with Ecclesiastes and (at least, in this author's opinion) those who have tried to do so have not been entirely convincing beyond something broad:

1. Introduction (1:1-1:11).
2. The meaninglessness of life, its various aspects – outside God (1:12-12:8).
3. Conclusion (12:9-12:14).

Some Bible translations provide, before what may be seen as sections, headings that suggest what to expect. As far as this book is concerned, these have proven useful, but this author will be not confined to any but they are given here for guidance purposes. This from the NIV is (again, in this author's opinion) helpful:

1. Everything is Meaningless (1:1-1:11).
2. Wisdom is Meaningless (1:12-1:18).
3. Pleasures are Meaningless (2:1-2:11).

4. Wisdom and Folly are Meaningless (2:12-2:16).
5. Toil is Meaningless (2:17-2:26).
6. A Time for Everything (3:1-3:22).
7. Oppression, Toil, Friendlessness (4:1-4:12).
8. Advancement is Meaningless (4:13-4:16).
9. Fulfil your Vow to God (5:1-5:7).
10. Riches are Meaningless (5:8-6:12).
11. Wisdom (7:1-8:1).
12. Obey the King (8:2-8:17).
13. A Common Destiny for All (9:1-9:12).
14. Wisdom Better than Folly (9:13-10:20).
15. Invest in many Ventures (11:1-11:6).
16. Remember your Creator while Young (11:7-12:8).
17. The Conclusion of the Matter (12:9-12:14).

Another credible attempt at breaking down the Book can be found in the New King James version breakdown, which while helpful is nevertheless incomplete still and is illustrative of how scholars can see things very differently. Readers are invited to attempt their own section titles but more importantly to come to grips with the essential message and main themes concerning life under the sun:

1. The Vanity of Life (1:1-1:11).
2. The Grief of Wisdom (1:12-1:18).
3. The Vanity of Pleasure (2:1-2:11).
4. The End of the Wise and the Fool (2:12-2:26).
5. Everything has its Time (3:1 – 3:15).
6. Injustice seems to Prevail (3:16-4:3).
7. The Vanity of Selfish Toil (4:4-4:8).
8. The Value of a Friend (4:9-4:16).
9. Fear God, Keep your Vows (5:1-5:7).
10. The Vanity of Gain and Honour (5:8-6:12).
11. The Value of Practical Wisdom (7:1-8:1).
12. Obey Authorities for God's Sake (8:2-8:9).
13. Death comes to us all (8:10-9:12).
14. Wisdom Superior to Folly (9:13-10:20).
15. The Value of Diligence (11:1-11:8).
16. Seek God Early in Life (11:9-12:8).
17. The Whole Duty of Man (12:9-12:14).

Just like Proverbs, there is an earthiness about Ecclesiastes that is refreshing. There is no beating about the bush when it comes to describing what the Teacher has seen and the matter-of-fact conclusion that, with or without religious piety, the fate of men could well be the same, regardless of their individual merits, and almost borders on the cynical (except that his approach was more that of a straight talker who pulls no punches). It should be borne in mind that some of what was set out could have just as easily been said by someone with no religious beliefs, because more often than not it was about life from a human, rather than a spiritual, perspective and, while seeming extreme, life looked at in this way often turns out a lottery. The key theme the Teacher often refers to is the meaninglessness (or pointlessness or vanity of vanities) of life under the sun, *i.e.* taking God out of the equation: "*Vanity of vanities, saith the Preacher, vanity of vanities; all is vanity. What profit hath a man of all his labour which he taketh under the sun?*" (1:2-3).

When I wrote on the Song of Songs and Proverbs, it was easy to know who to dedicate the books to – my wife in the former case and my son in the latter. Given Ecclesiastes was written from the perspective of a senior citizen – been there, done that, unshockable and all that, my thoughts turn to that older generation. There was a time, whenever I saw an old person, I found it difficult to imagine them in the prime of their youth – and that was a mistake, just as it was to dismiss them as old dodderers that fail to move with the times etc. One strange happening in recent years was meeting again with some of my former school mates. I last recalled many – full of bravado, mischief, confidence and ambition, soon to enter the workplace. When I met them again, they were about to retire or had retired, and the tell-tale signs of old age that had fallen on them was often all too evident. I would qualify my old person dedication to those who could say with Paul: "*I have fought a good fight, I have finished my course, I have kept the faith*" 2 Timothy 4:7, mindful that some like Solomon, started well but finished badly.

Some of that generation, which is now my generation (and the next to go – for as the Preacher reminds us – "*death is the end of all men*" (7:2)), are beset with health issues and some are struggling with some of the issues we typically associate with the elderly, including having succumbed to dementia. Many are married with children and grandchildren – some have lost their partner through bereavement or divorce. Looking over their lives, some have done well and amazing things, but for some life has been disappointing and unfulfilling. Some have discovered life under the sun is indeed meaningless without God, and some have even found Him. One of life's ironies is now of an age when getting what is going on, they may be ignored in societies that do not always respect the wisdom of the elderly. I dedicate this book to this elderly generation, especially those, however they are now, who have fought *the good fight of faith* (1 Timothy 6:12).

Approaching Ecclesiastes

Coming up with thirty-one daily meditations, in the case of Proverbs, was a challenge, although not in the same way when it came to sifting through hundreds of diverse "fortune cookies" and arranging under thirty-one headings, which we did with Proverbs. Ecclesiastes is at least more linked to a narrative, and can often be helpfully arranged in sections, albeit a lot of this is to do with the various aspects of meaninglessness. This creates a further challenge, for variations on the theme of the meaninglessness of life would not seem to be conducive when it comes to encouraging readers in their daily quiet times. But that can be a good thing as we can quickly dispense with the sugar coating. An attempt has been made to cover the main points of the Book, in a way that is meant to draw people away from dark thoughts and to give them inspiration and hope, under thirty-one headings – as to how successful this turns out to be, it is for readers to judge.

The following is based on notes found in my NIV Study Bible and what I have found from the Internet:

Solomon puts his wisdom to work to examine the human experience and assess the human situation. Although he sometimes brings God into it, notably in Chapters 3 and 12, he focuses on what happens *"under the sun"*. He considers life as he has experienced and observed it, between birth and death – life within the boundaries of this visible world. His wisdom cannot penetrate beyond that last horizon; he can only observe the phenomenon of death and perceive the limits it places on human beings. Within the limits of human experience and observation, he tries to spell out what is "good" for people to do, representing a devout wisdom. Life in the world is under God – for all its uncertainties and enigmas. Hence what begins with *"Vanity of vanities"* (1:2) ends with *"Remember your Creator"* (12:1) and *"Fear God and keep His commandments"* (12:13).

With a wisdom matured over many years and along with much experience, he takes the measure of human beings, examining their limits and their lot. He has attempted to see what human wisdom can do (1:13,16-18; 7:24; 8:16), and he has discovered that human wisdom, even when it has its beginning in *"the fear of the Lord"* (Proverbs 1:7), has limits to its powers when it attempts to go it alone – limits that circumscribe its perspectives and relativize its counsel. Most significantly, it cannot find out the larger purposes of God or the ultimate meaning of human existence. With respect to these it can only pose questions, and it does.

Nevertheless, Solomon does take a hard look at the human enterprise – an enterprise in which he himself has fully participated. He sees busy humans in pursuit of many different things, trying one thing after another, labouring away as if by human effort one could master the world, lay bare its deepest secrets, change its fundamental structures, burst through the bounds of human limitations, build enduring monuments, control one's destiny, achieve a state of secure and lasting happiness – people labouring at life with an overblown conception of human powers and consequently pursuing unrealistic hopes and aspirations. He takes a hard look and concludes human life is "meaningless"; its efforts all futile.

What the Teacher has learned includes:

1. Humans cannot by all their striving achieve anything of ultimate or enduring significance. Nothing appears to be going anywhere (1:5-11), and people cannot by all their efforts break out of this caged treadmill (1:2-4; 2:1-11); they cannot fundamentally change anything (1:12-15; 6:10; 7:13). Hence, they often toil foolishly (4:4,7-8; 5:10-17; 6:7-9). All their striving "under the sun" (1:3) after unreal goals leads only to disillusionment.
2. Wisdom is better than folly (2:13-14; 7:1-6,11-12,19; 8:1,5; 9:17-18; 10:1-3,12-15; 12:11) – it is God's gift to those who please him (2:26). But it is unwarranted to expect too much from having such wisdom – to expect that human wisdom is capable of solving all problems (1:16-18) or of securing for itself enduring rewards or advantages (2:12-17; 4:13-16; 9:13-16).
3. Experience confronts humans with many apparent disharmonies and anomalies that wisdom cannot unravel. Of these, the greatest is human life, which comes to the same end as that of the animals – death (2:15; 3:16-17; 7:15; 8:14; 9:1-3; 10:5-7).
4. Although God made humankind upright, people have gone in search of many "schemes" (to get ahead by taking advantage of others; see 7:29; cf. Psalm 10:2; 36:4; 140:2). So even humans are a disappointment (7:24-29).
5. People cannot know or control what will come after them, or even what lies in the more immediate future. Therefore, all their efforts remain balanced on the razor's edge of uncertainty (2:18; 6:12; 7:14; 9:2).
6. God keeps humans in their place (3:16-22).
7. God has ordered all things (3:1-15; 5:19; 6:1-6; 9:1), and a human being cannot change God's appointments or fully understand them or anticipate them (3:1; 7; 11:1-6). But the world is not fundamentally chaotic or irrational. It is ordered by God, and it is for humans to accept matters as they are by God's appointments, including their own limitations. Everything has its "time" and is good in its time.

He therefore counsels:

1. Accept the human state, as it is shaped by God's appointments and enjoy the life you have been given as fully as you can.
2. Don't trouble yourself with unrealistic goals – know the measure of

your human capabilities.
3. Be prudent in all your ways – follow wisdom's leading.
4. *"Fear God and keep his commandments"* (12:13), beginning in your youth before the fleeting days of life's enjoyments are gone and *"the days of trouble"* (12:1) come when the infirmities of advanced age vex you and hinder you from tasting, seeing and feeling the good things of life. While no kill joy, the Preacher stresses the need to fear God and to start young.
5. Ecclesiastes provides plentiful instruction on how to live meaningfully, purposefully and joyfully within the theocratic arrangement – primarily by placing God at the centre of one's life, work and activities, by contentedly accepting one's divinely appointed lot in life, by making sound life decisions and by reverently trusting in and obeying the Creator-King.

Interpreting Ecclesiastes

Ecclesiastes presents a naturalistic vision of life – seeing life through distinctively human eyes – but ultimately recognizes the rule and reign of God in the world. This more humanistic quality has made the book popular among certain audiences today, especially those who have seen more than their fair share of pain and instability in life but who still cling to their hope in God and can be recommended to any searching for meaning amidst meaninglessness. I suspect it also draws those who reject organised religion – because of its honesty. Whichever way you look at it, and Solomon gives several examples, life is pointless, but bring God into the picture and, while we may only see a small part, there is a point. Unlike Song of Songs, Bible scholars are broadly in agreement on how to interpret Ecclesiastes although, as this author has found out over a period of more than fifty years since discovering the book, there are many hidden depths to explore.

Ecclesiastes, like much of life, represents a journey from one point to another. Solomon articulated his starting point early in the book: "*Vanity of vanities, saith the Preacher, vanity of vanities; all is vanity. What profit hath a man of all his labour which he taketh under the sun?*" (1:2,3), indicating the utter futility and meaninglessness of life as he looked at it from under the sun as opposed to under heaven. Nothing made sense to him because he had already tried any number of remedies – pleasure, work, and intellect – to alleviate his sense of feeling lost in the world. All this makes depressing reading, but for God. Even so, and despite lots of good advice on how to make the most of our lot in life, this is no guarantee things will turn out well for us or better than with bad people or animals even.

In this important aspect, the optimism of Proverbs for those who follow the way of wisdom is not the picture presented in Ecclesiastes, other than God is for real and we should obey Him. In Solomon's search for meaning and significance in life, God remained present. For instance, we read God provides food, drink, and work (2:24); both the sinner and the righteous person live in God's sight (2:26); God's deeds are eternal (3:14); and God empowers people to enjoy His provision (5:19). Ultimately, the great truth of Ecclesiastes lies in the acknowledgment of God's ever-present hand on our lives. Even when injustice and uncertainty threaten to overwhelm us, we can (indeed must) trust and follow Him (12:13-14).

Not long after I became a Christian, as a teenager, I was invited to preach at the Gospel Meeting at my Brethren Assembly. I can't recall all the rationale or what I said on the occasion, but I chose to preach on Ecclesiastes, which is somewhat remarkable for someone just starting out, not expecting fifty years later I would find myself writing in-depth concerning this very book. I have discovered since then some preachers who have preached on this Book with a measure of success. I suggest for potential "soul winners" (which if we are Christian believers, we should be) the Book of Ecclesiastes may be a useful tool in our armoury because it so clearly conveys how life is under the sun. While it is not for us to question the ways of God, it is possible that its message that life is meaningless outside of God will have touched a chord with some. For those seeking to find out what life is about, Ecclesiastes may be a good place to start. Having woken to the notion of life's meaninglessness, we then turn to the Gospel which gives it meaning.

One might well argue that if life is a matter of pure chance, then the logical continuation is, it is indeed pointless. Regardless of whether or not one agrees with such a proposition, a sensible observer with a modicum of wisdom will have to conclude there is much in life that does not add up and a lot of it is unpredictable and unfair and is as much to do with chance and circumstances as talent, merit and careful planning. But if God were involved in the creation and sustaining of life (as Solomon clearly recognised), it is not unreasonable to want to explore the implications, and is what the Preacher of Ecclesiastes set out to do.

Knowingly or not, people have written profound stuff down the ages, at least suggesting a desire to find answers, around the theme of the meaning of life, where some of the ideas behind what they have written find their origin in the Book of Ecclesiastes, whether or not the authors realised it. I close this section with five quite different examples of such writings, where this was the case (imho), and leave readers to make the connection between these and Ecclesiastes.

From the "Hitchhikers Guide to the Galaxy" by Douglas Adams

"O Deep Thought computer," he said, "the task we have designed you to perform is this. We want you to tell us...." he paused, "The Answer."

"The Answer?" said Deep Thought. "The Answer to what?"

"Life!" urged Fook.

"The Universe!" said Lunkwill.

"Everything!" they said in chorus.

Deep Thought paused for a moment's reflection.

"Tricky," he said finally.

"But can you do it?"

Again, a significant pause.

"Yes," said Deep Thought, "I can do it."

"There is an answer?" said Fook with breathless excitement.

"Yes," said Deep Thought. "Life, the Universe, and Everything. There is an answer. But, I'll have to think about it."

...

Fook glanced impatiently at his watch.

"How long?" he said.

"Seven and a half million years," said Deep Thought.

Lunkwill and Fook blinked at each other.

"Seven and a half million years...!" they cried in chorus.

"Yes," declaimed Deep Thought, "I said I'd have to think about it, didn't I?"

From the popular hit musical "Cabaret"
"What good is sitting, alone in your room?
Come hear the music play!
Life is a cabaret, old chum!
Come to the cabaret!
Put down the knitting, the book and the broom
It's time for a holiday
Life is a cabaret, old chum!
Come to the cabaret!
...
And as for me
And as for me
I made my mind up back in Chelsea
When I go I'm going like Elsie.

Start by admitting
From cradle to tomb
It isn't that long a stay
Life is a cabaret, old chum!
It's only a cabaret, old chum!
And I love a cabaret!"

From "As you like it" by William Shakespeare
"All the world's a stage,
And all the men and women merely players;
They have their exits and their entrances,
And one man in his time plays many parts,
His acts being seven ages. At first, the infant,
Mewling and puking in the nurse's arms.
Then the whining schoolboy, with his satchel
And shining morning face, creeping like snail
Unwillingly to school. And then the lover,
Sighing like furnace, with a woeful ballad
Made to his mistress' eyebrow. Then a soldier,
Full of strange oaths and bearded like the pard,
Jealous in honor, sudden and quick in quarrel,
Seeking the bubble reputation
Even in the cannon's mouth. And then the justice,
In fair round belly with good capon lined,
With eyes severe and beard of formal cut,
Full of wise saws and modern instances;
And so he plays his part. The sixth age shifts
Into the lean and slippered pantaloon,
With spectacles on nose and pouch on side;

His youthful hose, well saved, a world too wide
For his shrunk shank, and his big manly voice,
Turning again toward childish treble, pipes
And whistles in his sound. Last scene of all,
That ends this strange eventful history,
Is second childishness and mere oblivion,
Sans teeth, sans eyes, sans taste, sans everything."

From the Rolling Stones hit – "Satisfaction"
"*I can't get no satisfaction*
I can't get no satisfaction
'Cause I try and I try and I try and I try
I can't get no, I can't get no
When I'm drivin' in my car
And a man comes on the radio
He's tellin' me more and more
About some useless information
Supposed to fire my imagination
…
When I'm ridin' round the world
And I'm doin' this and I'm signin' that
And I'm tryin' to make some girl
Who tells me baby better come back maybe next week
'Cause you see I'm on a losing streak

I can't get no
Oh no no no
Hey hey hey
That's what I say

I can't get no, I can't get no
I can't get no satisfaction
No satisfaction, no satisfaction
No satisfaction, I can't get no"

From the Order of Burial in the Book of Common Prayer (1662)
"*Man that is born of a woman hath but a short time to live, and is full of misery. He cometh up, and is cut down, like a flower; he fleeth as it were a shadow, and never continueth in one stay.*

In the midst of life we are in death: of whom may we seek for succour, but of thee, O Lord, who for our sins art justly displeased?

Yet, O Lord God most holy, O Lord most mighty, O holy and most merciful Saviour, deliver us not into the bitter pains of eternal death.

Thou knowest, Lord, the secrets of our hearts; shut not thy merciful ears to our prayer; but spare us, Lord most holy, O God most mighty, O holy and merciful Saviour, thou most worthy Judge eternal, suffer us not, at our last hour, for any pains of death, to fall from thee."

While the Preacher in Ecclesiastes was not in a position to preach what Christians understand as the Gospel (simply because it had not been revealed to him, although he did have glimpses), which does provide us with a meaning to life, he and we can likely identify with all five literary examples given above as relating to the message of the Book of Ecclesiastes. We can say there are answers, but before that it is important to recognise life that is lived out as under the sun is pointless and only becomes meaningful when God is brought into the picture.

Day 1: Vanity of vanities (1:3)

"The words of the Preacher, the son of David, king in Jerusalem. Vanity of vanities, saith the Preacher, vanity of vanities; all is vanity. What profit hath a man of all his labour which he taketh under the sun?"

We begin our journey through Ecclesiastes with three important considerations, which we will return to several times during the course of these daily reflections.

Firstly: there is the matter of the author, who identifies himself at the outset (and six times after that) as the Preacher (or Teacher), and was discussed in our introduction. While it is true, he is the son of King David (we assume Solomon), this is of lesser importance compared with his ability to teach and what it was he had to say. To be able to teach things so that listeners can benefit from learning, is a wonderful service that one is able to render to others. It is not one that should be under-estimated and, as far as the Preacher was concerned, he was well qualified to make the profound observations that he did. As a further thought, seeing life in the raw and experiencing disappointments can have its benefits.

Secondly: there is the recurring statement that *"all is vanity"* (everything is meaningless). In this first reference, it is to do with people's labours, for which they have toiled hard. This might come as a shock upon first hearing it, except it gets worse, as throughout the "sermon" more examples are cited concerning the vanity of life. As far as the Preacher was concerned, such labouring was pointless and, as we will soon see, so is almost all other human endeavour. Few of us take easily to the thought that our toil should not produce anything in terms of lasting gain, but that is precisely what happens when it is seen in purely human terms.

Thirdly: there is the other recurring statement: *"under the sun"*. It matters, for it indicates the Preacher is speaking from a human perspective, and does so when giving many of his further examples. We still have to wait patiently for when God is brought into the equation, for only then does life, which he otherwise regards as meaningless, becomes meaningful. The truth, which the Preacher was all too well aware of, is most people look at life from the perspective of "under the sun". With the benefit of years of experience and his God given wisdom, the Preacher could see what many value, under the illusion human endeavour has meaning, and discover to be pointless. Our challenge is: look beyond life under the sun to life above the sun, found in the unseen and sometimes incomprehensible spiritual world and, in any case, make the most of whatever our lot in life happens to be.

Prayer: We thank you Lord for the Preacher and his insights. Help us to be wise as far as living in this world is concerned and seek the wisdom that is from above.

Day 2: Nothing new under the sun (1:9)

"The thing that hath been, it is that which shall be; and that which is done is that which shall be done: and there is no new thing under the sun."

One way to view history is to see it as cyclic, *i.e.* history repeats itself. There are other ways to view history of course (arguably at least as valid) but that is the view of the Preacher. There really is nothing new under the sun as today's text will affirm, and all that takes place now has in some way happened in the past. The Preacher gives three examples of what we might describe as the cycle of nature. The sun sets and the sun also rises. The wind blows and, as it were, comes around and blows again. And then there is what we know as the water cycle – water flows from rivers, streams etc., into the sea and yet the sea is not full. We now understand the science behind all these repeated phenomena, but what is important here is these observations provide an entrée into his gloomy outlook on life. *"Everything leads to weariness – a weariness too great for words. Our eyes can never see enough to be satisfied; our ears can never hear enough"* (1:8 GNT). As far as the Preacher can make out, there is nothing new: *"No one remembers what has happened in the past, and no one in days to come will remember what happens between now and then"* (1:10 GNT). The sobering thought is: it is likely that for many of us, our grandchildren and those who come after them, will not spare us much thought or even remember us, and if you want evidence of that fact then consider how we view our not-so-distant ancestors and, as for learning the lessons of history, in the main that does not happen – bringing us back to our text.

Having set the scene, the Preacher introduces one of his main pre-occupations – the pursuit of knowledge and wisdom, but it does *not* have the same bright ending as when he discusses the subject in Proverbs. Having stated *"I determined that I would examine and study all the things that are done in this world"* (1:13 GNT), something many after him have set out to do, although it is unlikely with the same success, for he points out *"I know what wisdom and knowledge really are"* (1:16: GNT)), revealing his disappointment that *"everything done in this world, and I tell you, it is all useless. It is like chasing the wind"* (1:14 GNT). The sober ending to this is the observation he can do little to rectify the faults that are all too apparent and *"the wiser you are, the more worries you have; the more you know, the more it hurts"* (1:18 GNT) – and yet the question is begged (but not here – yet): is it better to be wise than foolish; to have knowledge than to be ignorant?

Prayer: We give to you Lord the pain we feel when we truly see what is going on around us and where all that is leading. May we not despise wisdom or knowledge, nor exalt it as the be all in life, and may our eyes be ever fixed on you.

Day 3: No profit under the sun (2:11)

"Then I looked on all the works that my hands had wrought, and on the labour that I had laboured to do: and, behold, all was vanity and vexation of spirit, and there was no profit under the sun."

If we think back to our younger days, for many, the driving force behind what we set out to do was pursuit of pleasure, and while some come to the same view, later in life, as had the Preacher, that it was all vanity, some will continue down this pointless path, right up to death. As far as the Preacher was concerned, he had tried it all, for being the king and having the power, there was nothing to stop him doing whatever caught his fancy and, looking back, there was much he did do and, unlike many who could only dream, he actually did all that he set out to do. After setting out his stall: "*I said in mine heart, go to now, I will prove thee with mirth, therefore enjoy pleasure*" albeit realising "*this also is vanity*" (2:1), he then goes and lists his many "achievements". He commissioned great works; he cultivated beautiful gardens; he was able to amass much wealth; he possessed large flocks and herds; he could be entertained any way he wanted, including having his own musicians and singers; he could have any woman he wanted; he acquired many possessions – the wherewithal to pay was no obstacle. There was no end to what he wanted and got and he still managed to hang on to his great wisdom. Having listed all he could, he could declare: "*Yes, I was great, greater than anyone else who had ever lived in Jerusalem, and my wisdom never failed me. Anything I wanted, I got. I did not deny myself any pleasure. I was proud of everything I had worked for, and all this was my reward. Then I thought about all that I had done and how hard I had worked doing it, and I realized that it didn't mean a thing. It was like chasing the wind – of no use at all*" (2:9-11 GNT).

It is sometimes reckoned that the pursuit of pleasure and sensual self-indulgence is what defines the overriding philosophy in the lives of many. We have here a list of achievements that most of us can only dream about. But the Preacher saw the end of it all and it was pointless. The challenge for us concerns priorities. It is not that a lot of what he did was wrong *per se* but rather making these his goals in life. We await to see what he thought should be our priorities but for the time being we should ponder the words of Jesus: "*But lay up for yourselves treasures in heaven, where neither moth nor rust doth corrupt, and where thieves do not break through nor steal ... But seek ye first the kingdom of God, and his righteousness; and all these things shall be added unto you*" Matthew 6:20,33.

Prayer: We thank you Lord for the good things in life we can enjoy. Forgive us for making these our main goal. May we seek your kingdom and righteousness.

Day 4: Eat, drink and enjoy (2:24)

"There is nothing better for a man, than that he should eat and drink, and that he should make his soul enjoy good in his labour. This also I saw, that it was from the hand of God."

There is no let up, after establishing that a life of pleasure is pointless. Having acknowledged there was not much he could do following what his predecessor had done to make the most of life under the sun, the Preacher does concede *"that wisdom excelleth folly, as far as light excelleth darkness"* (2:13), yet despite that *"as it happeneth to the fool, so it happeneth even to me and why was I then more wise?"* (2:15). Rather gloomily it seems, he picks up on the same point he made in Chapter 1 – the end of the wise and the fool is the same – death, and very soon after that no-one could tell one from the other or even care. He then comes to a rather sombre view: *"Therefore I hated life; because the work that is wrought under the sun is grievous unto me: for all is vanity and vexation of spirit"* (2:17).

Then he comes to a preoccupation many of us can identify with – the significance of working hard, making the best use of our wisdom, knowledge, and skill, and when it comes to taking a view on accumulating wealth. In the end, we leave what we have to someone who has not earned it and quite possibly to someone who is foolish. While we may dispute the Preacher's conclusion and argue making good use of our talents etc., is a laudable goal, yet it is still difficult to dispute – *"For what hath man of all his labour, and of the vexation of his heart, wherein he hath laboured under the sun? For all his days are sorrows, and his travail grief; yea, his heart taketh not rest in the night. This is also vanity"* (2:22,23). While a more optimistic response is possible when God is brought into the equation, we can begin by going from pessimism to realism, which brings us to today's text: *"The best thing we can do is eat and drink and enjoy what we have earned. And yet, I realized that even this comes from God. How else could you have anything to eat or enjoy yourself at all?"* (2:24,25 GNT.) We could take this as a pragmatic view of life. There is a song by one, Bobby McFerrin, that goes *"Don't worry, be happy, in every life we have some trouble, but when you worry you make it double, don't worry, be happy, don't worry, be happy now"* who seems to take a similar view of life. As for the Preacher, he ends on a positive note: *"For God giveth to a man that is good in his sight wisdom, and knowledge, and joy: but to the sinner he giveth travail, to gather and to heap up, that he may give to him that is good before God. This also is vanity and vexation of spirit"* (2:26).

Prayer: We thank you Lord that your word pulls no punches when it comes to viewing our own labours, but we thank you when we can enjoy the fruits thereof.

Day 5: To everything there is a season (3:1)

"To everything there is a season, and a time to every purpose under the heaven."
"A time to be born, and a time to die; a time to plant, and a time to pluck up that which is planted; A time to kill, and a time to heal; a time to break down, and a time to build up; A time to weep, and a time to laugh; a time to mourn, and a time to dance; A time to cast away stones, and a time to gather stones together; a time to embrace, and a time to refrain from embracing; A time to get, and a time to lose; a time to keep, and a time to cast away; A time to rend, and a time to sew; a time to keep silence, and a time to speak; A time to love, and a time to hate; a time of war, and a time of peace" (3:2-8).

Today we consider the Preacher's proposition: *"Everything that happens in this world happens at the time God chooses"* (3:1 GNT). We reflect on the declaration there is a time to do this and to do that, where "this" and "that" are polar opposites and there are 14 very different "this" and "that" examples. Before we consider each pair, it is worth reflecting life under the sun is time bound and the older we get the more we notice how time does fly and how often we do not make best use of time, and often what we do or don't do is dictated by life's circumstances. Our challenge is to make best use of the short time we have and wise up as to when we should do something or, in the light of these examples, the opposite, although, also in the light of these examples, we don't always have a choice in the matter. We do well *"Redeeming the time, because the days are evil"* Ephesians 5:16.

1. That we are born and die are facts of life, applying to us all, we can't change.
2. As much as we may want to reap a harvest, before that we need to sow a seed.
3. We are likely agreed healing is a needful thing, but killing may be inevitable.
4. We build, including on what is there, but sometimes we have to first tear down.
5. A fact of life is things happen to bring us sorrow, as much as to bring us joy.
6. Continuing on … some things give rise to mourning but some to dancing.
7. Stones may be materials used for building, or impediments to soil fertility.
8. Making love is one of the great pleasures of life, but often we must refrain.
9. Gaining and losing are facts of life, either done through choice or imposed.
10. Similarly – when it comes to saving or throwing away what we have.
11. Similarly – when it comes to tearing up what we have or mending it.
12. The biggie for many of us … knowing when to speak and when to be silent.
13. While love should be what defines us, we are also called to hate what is evil.
14. Peace is better than war; let's work for peace, but war may be unavoidable.

Prayer: We thank you Lord that what happens in this world happens in your perfect time. Forgive us for wasting time and help us use our time wisely.

Day 6: Discovering the works of God (3:11)

"He hath made every thing beautiful in his time: also he hath set the world in their heart, so that no man can find out the work that God maketh from the beginning to the end."

Yesterday, we reflected on the Preacher's assertion *"there is a season, and a time to every purpose under the heaven"* and 14 examples of when to do something and 14 examples of when to do the opposite. Now we ponder concerning where all this is leading us: *"What do we gain from all our work? I know the heavy burdens that God has laid on us. He has set the right time for everything. He has given us a desire to know the future, but never gives us the satisfaction of fully understanding what he does. So I realized that all we can do is be happy and do the best we can while we are still alive. All of us should eat and drink and enjoy what we have worked for. It is God's gift."* (3:9-13 GNT.) Having made the argument life under the sun is meaningless, and asking what it is we gain from our efforts and pondering the burden of daily living, he looks beyond the sun, and brings God into the picture, and then things make more sense. That God makes *everything beautiful in his time* is a precious thought, despite man's efforts to spoil what God has made. So is the notion we are in the image of God and desirous to know the future, albeit never with full understanding. He points out that it is ok to be happy and do the best we can, referring back to an earlier conclusion (2:24) that we can eat, drink and enjoy, for that is how God had intended it for us.

Despite the inevitability that life is cyclic and, what we do now, people will do in the future and is what others have done in the past, but we can still look to God. Indeed, we should, as what God does lasts forever; that is a good thing because it is right *"that men should fear before him"* (3:14): *"I know that everything God does will last forever. You can't add anything to it or take anything away from it. And one thing God does is to make us stand in awe of him. Whatever happens or can happen has already happened before. God makes the same thing happen again and again."* (3:14-15 GNT.) One of the refreshing comments we can make about the Book of Ecclesiastes is that the Preacher cuts to the proverbial chase and does what our culture discourages us from doing – to have a good hard look at life under the sun but then to look beyond that and invite God into our lives and live out our lives standing in awe of Him, and then it begins to make sense.

Prayer: We thank you Lord that you make everything beautiful in your time, all that you do will last forever regardless of what we do, and you give us a desire to understand the world and your eternal purposes. Forgive us for viewing life merely as what takes place under the sun and help us to stand in awe of you.

Day 7: Injustice in the world (3:22)

"Wherefore I perceive that there is nothing better, than that a man should rejoice in his own works; for that is his portion: for who shall bring him to see what shall be after him?"

We ended yesterday's reflection with the positive and negative consequences of *"whatever happens or can happen has already happened before"* (3:15 GNT). The Preacher continues, noting: *"that in this world you find wickedness where justice and right ought to be"* (3:16 GNT). When you think about it, this is a pretty damning statement, especially if you live in a country that purports to uphold the rule of law. The reality is something that the Psalmist observed – not only does wickedness happen when there ought to be justice and right, but often the wicked appear to get away with it, scot-free, and this can happen anywhere, including in the places where the Preacher was the king! We may console ourselves with thoughts that are only valid if there is more than what goes on under the sun: *"God is going to judge the righteous and the evil alike"* (3:17 GNT) and *"that God is testing us, to show us that we are no better than animals"* (3:18 GNT) but it is naturally worrying to think what happens, if all there is, is life under the sun.

How many times we have heard these words from the Order of Burial Service from the 1662 Prayer Book ... *"Forasmuch as it hath pleased Almighty God of his great mercy to take unto himself the soul of our dear brother here departed, we therefore commit his body to the ground; earth to earth, ashes to ashes, dust to dust; in sure and certain hope of the Resurrection to eternal life, through our Lord Jesus Christ ..."*? The first part reiterates what the Preacher said: *"All go unto one place; all are of the dust, and all turn to dust again"* (3:20), but not the rest. He asks the question that reveals how meaningless life truly is, which in this instance is about unrequited injustice: *"Who knoweth the spirit of man that goeth upward, and the spirit of the beast that goeth downward to the earth?"* (3:21). Given this and taking God out of the equation (although the wisdom may apply even if He is put back in), we come to today's text as a *modus operandi* in coming to terms with life under the sun: *"So I realized then that the best thing we can do is enjoy what we have worked for. There is nothing else we can do. There is no way for us to know what will happen after we die"* (GNT). We who trust in Jesus know what will happen after we die, but to work for the right things with the right motives and enjoying the fruits of our labours is something we can do and enjoy.

Prayer: We confess Lord we are perplexed when we *find wickedness where justice and right ought to be* but we know all men will have to give an account of their actions on the Day of Judgement. Thank you we can rejoice in the things we can do and know that you are a just, all powerful God, who does all things well.

Day 8: The oppression of the oppressed (4:1)

"So I returned, and considered all the oppressions that are done under the sun: and behold the tears of such as were oppressed, and they had no comforter; and on the side of their oppressors there was power; but they had no comforter."

The subject of justice, especially for the poor, weak, disempowered, vulnerable, bothered the Preacher, as we considered yesterday. He saw that the cards stacked against the oppressed and, as for the oppressors, they not only held the upper hand, but exploited their position. To make things worse, the oppressed had no-one to help them – they were victims with none to rescue them. It should be noted such a scenario was a far cry from that envisaged under the Law of Moses, where special provision was made to look after those who might fall victim to being oppressed, but then we are reminded we are speaking of life under the sun.

When we consider the Prophets of the Bible, they had many complaints but one that often featured, because it came from the heart of God, was when such people were oppressed and that justice, they should count on, was denied. The Psalmist could see what was happening and what was needed: *"How long will ye judge unjustly, and accept the persons of the wicked? Selah. Defend the poor and fatherless: do justice to the afflicted and needy. Deliver the poor and needy: rid them out of the hand of the wicked"* Psalm 82:2-4. Things were so bad that the Preacher could say: *"I envy those who are dead and gone; they are better off than those who are still alive. But better off than either are those who have never been born, who have never seen the injustice that goes on in this world"* (4:2,3 GNT).

It is a subject that ought to concern God's people today. It is not just one for those of a more liberal persuasion to claim the moral higher ground, but also for those who believe preaching the gospel of repentance and personal holiness should be our priority. We are required to follow the Great Command of *"love thy neighbour"* and should recall the words of Him who is the centre of the gospel, who lived a perfectly holy life: *"The Spirit of the Lord God is upon me; because the Lord hath anointed me to preach good tidings unto the meek; he hath sent me to bind up the brokenhearted, to proclaim liberty to the captives, and the opening of the prison to them that are bound; To proclaim the acceptable year of the Lord, and the day of vengeance of our God; to comfort all that mourn"* Isaiah 61:1-2. Here is not the place to spell out how we should respond to the call to comfort the oppressed, but we are responsible for finding and making the right response.

Prayer: Dear Lord, we cry to you with righteous anger because of the cries of the oppressed. Forgive us when we ignore those cries. Help us to respond aright.

Day 9: The quiet life (4:6)

"Better is an handful with quietness, than both the hands full with travail and vexation of spirit."

The Preacher turns to yet another vanity – expending one's efforts to succeed – all in order to keep up with the Joneses. *"I have also learned why people work so hard to succeed: it is because they envy the things their neighbors have. But it is useless. It is like chasing the wind. They say that we would be fools to fold our hands and let ourselves starve to death. Maybe so, but it is better to have only a little, with peace of mind, than be busy all the time with both hands, trying to catch the wind"* (4:4-6 GNT). If we are honest with ourselves, a lot of our motivation and prioritisation behind doing the things we do may be because we see others do it (herd instinct if you will) and we want to be like them, or even better.

As far as the Preacher was concerned – this is folly, when considering the high price that needs to be paid – *"The fool foldeth his hands together, and eateth his own flesh"*. It is sometimes said that we live in a dog-eat-dog world, where people do whatever it takes to be successful, even if it means harming others, but that was the very world, then and now, we should avoid, even if it means having only a little. With respect to today's text, a *"handful with quietness"* is better than having *"both the hands full with travail and vexation of spirit"*. We conclude, if seen in such a light that when it comes to working hard to succeed with the wrong motives: *"This also is vanity and a striving after wind"* (4:4 ESV). One question begged is: "where should our efforts be directed"? One thing we conclude from what the Preacher tells us is that it shouldn't be in following the crowd or out of envy of things others have that we don't, or trying to impress other people. That is where life under the sun might take us, but as people of God we should be looking beyond the sun. Working hard for the right reasons is a good thing. On a basic level, it provides us with the wherewithal to sustain life and that of our dependants. It may even give us excess such that we can use it to bless other people. And come to think of it, is not enjoying a quiet life where we can enjoy the little we do have better than an unquiet life where we don't enjoy the excess that we have. And beyond that, as people of God, we are not here to be beholden to the priorities of others, many of which will not give God the time of the day, but rather we are called to *"seek ye first the kingdom of God, and his righteousness; and all these things shall be added unto you"* Matthew 6:33.

Prayer: Forgive us Lord when we envy what others have and toil hard for the wrong things and with the wrong motives. Rather may we seek your kingdom and your righteousness and may we work hard to honour you and bless others.

Day 10 The Desirability of Companionship (4:9)

"Two are better than one; because they have a good reward for their labour."

Following yesterday's reflection on the pointlessness of labouring hard for wrong reasons, the Preacher considers a related scenario – when someone works hard and denies himself in the process, but there is no-one with whom he can share the fruits of his labours: *"I have noticed something else in life that is useless. Here is someone who lives alone. He has no son, no brother, yet he is always working, never satisfied with the wealth he has. For whom is he working so hard and denying himself any pleasure? This is useless, too – and a miserable way to live."* (4:7,8 GNT.) On the theme of aloneness and the desirability of companionship, we come to today's text, followed by the rationale as to why that is the case: *"Two are better off than one, because together they can work more effectively. If one of them falls down, the other can help him up. But if someone is alone and falls, it's just too bad, because there is no one to help him. If it is cold, two can sleep together and stay warm, but how can you keep warm by yourself. Two people can resist an attack that would defeat one person alone. A rope made of three cords is hard to break."* (4:9-12 GNT.)

Today, we consider the importance of sharing our life with someone and the pitfalls when going it alone. It has always been God's intention we make time and take effort to relate to and interact with others, and first and foremost with our spouse, parents and children. Life often reveals examples of when these relationships break down or don't happen. One reason for this is when one's priority is one's work and other interests, at the cost of relationship building. This includes single people who may be free from family responsibilities yet may have opportunities to cultivate relationships denied to married people. Some see themselves as "loners", and find close relationship building something that is difficult. But it is clear, as far as the Preacher is concerned, building good relations reaps dividends and is worth the effort. In many situations, two is better than one for practical reasons. The Preacher ends by painting another picture – *"Someone may rise from poverty to become king of his country, or go from prison to the throne, but if in his old age he is too foolish to take advice, he is not as well off as a young man who is poor but intelligent … There may be no limit to the number of people a king rules; when he is gone, no one will be grateful for what he has done. It is useless. It is like chasing the wind."* (4:13-14, 16 GNT) How tragic – this old, foolish king has gone from rags to riches, is unwilling to take advice, and he isolates himself. His place is taken by someone like he had once been. When the king is gone, there is no-one around to honour him.

Prayer: Forgive us Lord when our priorities are wrong and we fail to look out for other people, whether our spouse, children and parents or people we come across. May we see the folly of going it alone and the wisdom of sharing with other people.

Day 11: Attitudes toward God (5:1)

"Keep thy foot when thou goest to the house of God, and be more ready to hear, than to give the sacrifice of fools: for they consider not that they do evil."

Today's "verse" is part of a section, verses 1 through 7, given a variety of titles: "Don't Make Rash Promises (GNT)", "Fear God (ESV)", "God's in Charge, Not You (MSG)", "Fulfil Your Vow to God (NIV)" and, appropriately, for today's thoughts: "Your Attitude Toward God" (AMP, NASB). Solomon was well qualified to make his observations despite, in later life, *not* practising what he preached. It was he, who was the main instigator behind building the main "house of God" – the Temple, and he even built his own house in the best spot possible – next door, giving him easy access to the Temple, where he could view "worshippers" coming and going. Likely, he saw in many cases it was a sham. Jesus told of a Pharisee and Tax collector, Luke 18:11-14. *"The Pharisee stood by himself and prayed this prayer: 'I thank you, God, that I am not like other people – cheaters, sinners, adulterers. I'm certainly not like that tax collector! I fast twice a week, and I give you a tenth of my income.' "But the tax collector stood at a distance and dared not even lift his eyes to heaven as he prayed. Instead, he beat his chest in sorrow, saying, 'O God, be merciful to me, for I am a sinner.' I tell you, this sinner, not the Pharisee, returned home justified before God. For those who exalt themselves will be humbled, and those who humble themselves will be exalted."* John Bunyan understood well what is needed: *"When you pray, rather let your heart be without words than your words without heart"*.

We need to have the right attitude when we approach God. As Jesus reminds us: *"These people draw near to Me with their mouth, And honour Me with their lips, But their heart is far from Me"* Matthew 15:8. God is not interested in lip service, however elaborate that is, or eloquent the language we use – God is more interested in the language of the heart and the seriousness of how we carry out doing what He requires from us. Jesus also said: *"But let your communication be, Yea, yea; Nay, nay: for whatsoever is more than these cometh of evil"* Matthew 5:37. This brings us to the subject of promises and vows, something that was an important part of ancient Hebrew worship that people were required to carry out, under penalty if they did not, and which is arguably ever applicable. We round off this section with a reminder of what is needed and of something the Preacher saw was absent then and would likely do so if he were considering religious attitudes in our own times: *"For in many dreams and in many words there is futility. Rather, fear God"* (5:7 NASB.) We are told *"to obey is better than sacrifice"* 1 Samuel 15:22 and that *"God is a Spirit: and they that worship him must worship him in spirit and in truth"* John 4:24.

Prayer: Dear Lord, forgive us when we approach worshipping you, the Almighty God, without the honour you deserve. May we come to you with the right attitude.

Day 12: Attitudes toward money (5:10,11)

"He that loveth silver shall not be satisfied with silver; nor he that loveth abundance with increase. When goods increase, they are increased that eat them: and what good is there to the owners thereof, saving the beholding of them with their eyes?"

Before we consider the subject of attitudes toward money, which dominate the rest of the chapter, one way or another, we consider something that is strangely related – attitudes toward the poor, which is something we have already seen on our journey through Ecclesiastes and, before that, Proverbs: *"If thou seest the oppression of the poor, and violent perverting of judgment and justice in a province, marvel not at the matter: for he that is higher than the highest regardeth; and there be higher than they"* (5:8). In a way, poverty and money, or rather the lack of money, are related. Here it is the Preacher's matter of fact observation *"that the government oppresses the poor and denies them justice and their rights. Every official is protected by someone higher, and both are protected by still higher officials"* (5:8 GNT). While we shouldn't be surprised because that is the way things are, it should be cause for concern and something to exercise our conscience, in knowing how best to respond.

Back to money – as the song from the musical "Cabaret" reminds us: *"Money makes the world go around, the world go around, the world go around; money makes the world go around, it makes the world go round"*. Money is a driving force behind so much that goes on under the sun. Money has positive aspects, such as noted by John Wesley: *"Earn all you can, give all you can, save all you can"*, but more on that tomorrow. For now, we will reflect on the negative aspects. Money does not satisfy; the more we have the more we want and, unlike those who do not have money, we might spend an inordinate amount of time worrying because of it. Accumulation of wealth is subject to the uncertainties of life – we are just as likely to lose the money we have as we are to acquire more of it. Besides the Preacher's salutary observation of the untoward effects of how it is when people love money, the Bible is full of warnings against making money a personal driving force: *"For the love of money is the root of all evil: which while some coveted after, they have erred from the faith, and pierced themselves through with many sorrows"* 1 Timothy 6:10. The priorities that should guide our life decisions can be seen in the words of Jesus: *"Lay not up for yourselves treasures upon earth, where moth and rust doth corrupt, and where thieves break through and steal: But lay up for yourselves treasures in heaven, where neither moth nor rust doth corrupt, and where thieves do not break through nor steal: For where your treasure is, there will your heart be also"* Matthew 6:19-21.

Prayer: Free us dear Lord from the love of money and forgive us for being sucked in to wanting to become rich when you call us to seek first your kingdom and your righteousness, knowing that the things that truly matter shall then be added unto us.

Day 13: Attitudes toward death (5:15,16)

"As he came forth of his mother's womb, naked shall he return to go as he came, and shall take nothing of his labour, which he may carry away in his hand. And this also is a sore evil, that in all points as he came, so shall he go: and what profit hath he that hath laboured for the wind?"

One thing we can be certain: we will die; just as we came into the world with nothing, we will leave it in the same way. The observations of the Preacher are pertinent: "*We go just as we came. We labor, trying to catch the wind, and what do we get? We get to live our lives in darkness and grief, worried, angry, and sick.*" (5:16,17 GNT.) Despite this sobering prospect, he follows on his sombre reflecting on the subject of acquisition of wealth on a positive note, repeating some conclusions he had made earlier in his "sermon": "*Behold that which I have seen: it is good and comely for one to eat and to drink, and to enjoy the good of all his labour that he taketh under the sun all the days of his life, which God giveth him: for it is his portion. Every man also to whom God hath given riches and wealth, and hath given him power to eat thereof, and to take his portion, and to rejoice in his labour; this is the gift of God. For he shall not much remember the days of his life; because God answereth him in the joy of his heart*" (5:18-20). As for balance, consider Paul's words: "*Charge them that are rich in this world, that they be not highminded, nor trust in uncertain riches, but in the living God, who giveth us richly all things to enjoy*" 1 Timothy 6:17.

It is important to reach the right balance such as represented in yesterday's "*Earn all you can, give all you can, save all you can*" quote. We are called to be good stewards who need to make wise use of whatever the Lord entrusts to us, and this can be seen in our shared experience – we work and are rewarded financially, begging the question: what to do next? Other than not misusing that money or excessive indulgence, we are free to do what we will, according to our conscience and what is right. The Preacher's matter of fact counsel is to enjoy what we have: "*Here is what I have found out: the best thing we can do is eat and drink and enjoy what we have worked for during the short life that God has given us; this is our fate. If God gives us wealth and property and lets us enjoy them, we should be grateful and enjoy what we have worked for. It is a gift from God. Since God has allowed us to be happy, we will not worry too much about how short life is.*" (5:18-20 GNT). The rich-poor divide is as great now as it ever was in Solomon's day, and it is unlikely we can do much to change that – but we can do something. The right approach to money is to see it merely as a commodity we can use to bless others and thankfully remember, while not trusting in our money, God gives us *richly all things to enjoy.*

Prayer: Lord help us have the right view to money – not trust in it but to be thankful for what we have and enjoy it, but also to use it wisely and in blessing others.

Day 14: Content with our lot in life (6:1,2)

"There is an evil which I have seen under the sun, and it is common among men: A man to whom God hath given riches, wealth, and honour, so that he wanteth nothing for his soul of all that he desireth, yet God giveth him not power to eat thereof, but a stranger eateth it: this is vanity, and it is an evil disease."

The Preacher reflects on something that is *common among men* – they may get all they ever want (and, incidentally, it is because God gives to them) but they are unable to enjoy the *riches, wealth, and honour* that has been given. The truth of the matter is, because fallen man does not put his confidence in God, he finds it necessary to put his confidence in something. Often, this "something" includes material wealth. The Preacher paints a depressing picture of a man with many children, who are not around to give him a good send off when he is dead, and the man who lives a long (2000 years) life. He is likened to a still born baby: "*It never sees the light of day or knows what life is like, but at least it has found rest – more so than the man who never enjoys life*" (6:5,6 GNT). He concludes: "*We do all our work just to get something to eat, but we never have enough. How are the wise better off than fools? What good does it do the poor to know how to face life? It is useless; it is like chasing the wind. It is better to be satisfied with what you have than to be always wanting something else.*" (6:7-9 GNT.)

The key thought is contentment, and we should be content with what we have and with God. Like J. N. Darby, at the end of his life, we might say: "*He is all we want ... I can look back and see a patience and a faithfulness, a goodness beyond all my thoughts*". We might echo the words of the hymn: "*All good gifts around us, are sent from Heaven above, so thank the Lord, oh, thank the Lord for all His love*". Then there was the rich young ruler who preferred treasure on earth more than in heaven (Mark 10:21). But we will let the Apostle Paul have the last word, which is a commentary on today's text and others given earlier by the Preacher: "*Not that I speak in respect of want: for I have learned, in whatsoever state I am, therewith to be content*" Philippians 4:11. Also, "*But godliness with contentment is great gain. For we brought nothing into this world, and it is certain we can carry nothing out. And having food and raiment let us be therewith content. But they that will be rich fall into temptation and a snare, and into many foolish and hurtful lusts, which drown men in destruction and perdition. For the love of money is the root of all evil: which while some coveted after, they have erred from the faith, and pierced themselves through with many sorrows*" 1 Timothy 6:6-10.

Prayer: Thank you Lord for what we have and help us to be content with it. May we be found ever seeking you and living our life in order to bring you glory.

Day 15: The uncertainties of life (6:12)

"For who knoweth what is good for man in this life, all the days of his vain life which he spendeth as a shadow? for who can tell a man what shall be after him under the sun?"
"Everything that happens was already determined long ago, and we all know that you cannot argue with someone who is stronger than you. The longer you argue, the more useless it is, and you are no better off. How can anyone know what is best for us in this short, useless life of ours – a life that passes like a shadow? How can we know what will happen in the world after we die?" (6:10-12 GNT.)

The one thing in life we can be certain of is that it is short– ask someone who has reached three score years and ten and they will confirm how quickly their life has passed and that during the course of that life, regardless of whether or not one has planned what was to happen, there were uncertainties and unexpected events that had a bearing, and likely many of them, and all of which will take us off in directions we can hardly imagine. Everything that happens has been long ago determined and, however we may try to argue, we are unable to make much of a difference, begging the question is there a lot more to life than what goes on under the sun? Knowing what is best for us is also a challenge, for the Preacher argues we not only do not know but we cannot know. As for life, it is short and useless (vain) and, in the bigger scheme of things, it passes like a mere shadow and we are relatively insignificant nobodies. As for what will happen to the world when we depart from it, according to the Preacher, we are not in a position to say, other than life goes on. All of which makes depressing reading, and while he has made suggestions of how to make the most of our "miserable" existence, we have to wait to the final chapter to make significant sense of how things can be for us. Given life is short, full of uncertainties and there is so much in life that we have little control over, the question is – what are we going to do about it? We need look no further than the words of Jesus and His call upon our lives to be true disciples of His, but this needs us to recognise there is only true purpose in life beyond the sun: *"And when he had called the people unto him with his disciples also, he said unto them, Whosoever will come after me, let him deny himself, and take up his cross, and follow me. For whosoever will save his life shall lose it; but whosoever shall lose his life for my sake and the gospel's, the same shall save it. For what shall it profit a man, if he shall gain the whole world, and lose his own soul? Or what shall a man give in exchange for his soul"* (Mark 8:34-37)?

Prayer: Thank you for reminding us that life is short and uncertain and we cannot even tell what will come next, but we can follow you Lord. Please help us do so.

Day 16: A better way to live (7:5,8)

"It is better to hear the rebuke of the wise, than for a man to hear the song of fools ... Better is the end of a thing than the beginning thereof: and the patient in spirit is better than the proud in spirit."

In the first six (artificial) chapters of Ecclesiastes, the Preacher provides many powerful examples of why life under the sun is meaningless. He turns his attention to what was his principal theme in the Book of Proverbs – the way of wisdom, and goes on to provide several examples of why that is the way we should be following. But first he considers what is better as opposed to what is worse. As for examples (which we can identify with), that on the face of it appear random, we can cite seven from the first eight verses of Chapter 7 (GNT). We then ask seven questions, which if nothing else will challenge our priorities:

*v1 A good reputation is **better** than expensive perfume; and the day you die is better than the day you are born.*

*v2 It is **better** to go to a home where there is mourning than to one where there is a party, because the living should always remind themselves that death is waiting.*

*v3 Sorrow is **better** than laughter; it may sadden your face, but it sharpens your understanding.*

*v5 It is **better** to have wise people reprimand you than to have stupid people sing your praises.*

*v8 The end of something is **better** than its beginning. Patience is better than pride.*

1. Rather than the "sweet" trappings of wealth, should not our focus be on becoming good, faithful, honourable people?
2. We may look back on our coming into the world but would we not do better to think about how we are to leave the world?
3. The natural desire of human kind is to want to have a good time etc., (party) but should we not rather be living in the light of eternity?
4. Most of us like a good laugh (it is after all an agreeable distraction) but given the reality of life, would we not do better to have sorrow?
5. We may love to be praised – but should we not prefer it if we are told when we are going wrong – because it may help make us better people?
6. However good or bad something is at the beginning, isn't the ending more important and should not our strategy in life be to affect a good ending?
7. Should we not value patience as an antidote to pride?

Prayer: We thank you Lord, you want us to follow the better way. We are faced with so many decisions and temptations. Help us choose what is pleasing to you. May we not even be satisfied with good or even better, but rather best – your best.

Day 17: It is back to wisdom (7:19)

"Wisdom strengtheneth the wise more than ten mighty men which are in the city."

We change tack from what is better to what is wise, with advice reminiscent of *"be ye angry, and sin not"* Ephesians 4:26, and a reminder of how to respond, when inevitably someone or something upsets us: *"Be not hasty in thy spirit to be angry: for anger resteth in the bosom of fools"* (7:9). We may be right to be angry if we feel hurt or see unrighteousness, but we need wisdom in how to respond. Just as yesterday when we tried to learn the lessons whenever the word "better" was used, so today we do the same with the word "wise", bearing in mind, as with 7:9, what the Preacher had to say for much of the rest of Ecclesiastes, was about the way of wisdom, regardless of whether that word was used. We are back once again to *"Wisdom is the principal thing; therefore get wisdom"* Proverbs 4:7.

v10 Say not thou, What is the cause that the former days were better than these? for thou dost not enquire wisely concerning this. There is a tendency for older people, especially, to hark back to the good old days – but that is not being wise.

v11 **Wisdom** *is good with an inheritance: and by it there is profit to them that see the sun.* While material wealth, *e.g.* as part of an inheritance, is not to be sought after yet, when its use is coupled with wisdom, it can be a good thing.

v12 For **wisdom** *is a defence, and money is a defence: but the excellency of knowledge is, that* **wisdom** *giveth life to them that have it.* Again, while not discounting the usefulness of money, wisdom is better, for it gives life.

v16 Be not righteous over much; neither make thyself over **wise***: why shouldest thou destroy thyself?* How often do we do this? Simply put – we shouldn't.

v19 **Wisdom** *strengtheneth the wise more than ten mighty men which are in the city.* We want strength to withstand attack, but wisdom is the best way to do it.

v23 All this have I proved by **wisdom***: I said, I will be wise; but it was far from me.* Concerning doing the right thing and what people say about us behind our back or in front of our face, the best response is wisdom – but it isn't easy.

v25 I applied mine heart to know, and to search, and to seek out **wisdom***, and the reason of things, and to know the wickedness of folly, even of foolishness and madness.* Which is a good approach to life and is also our text for tomorrow!

Prayer: Thank you Lord for reminding us of the importance of wisdom, as we try to come to terms with life under the sun. Forgive us for not seeking wisdom and may we now apply our heart to know, and to search, and to seek out wisdom.

Day 18: The meaning of life (7:25)

"I applied mine heart to know, and to search, and to seek out wisdom, and the reason of things, and to know the wickedness of folly, even of foolishness and madness."

We left our yesterday thought, which was all about wisdom and how desirable having it was, with today's text. But before we unravel this and what follows, it is worth reflecting on the text preceding: *"That which is far off, and exceeding deep, who can find it out?"* (7:24), or put slightly differently: *"How can anyone discover what life means? It is too deep for us, too hard to understand"* (7:24 GNT). Since the beginning of human existence, people have tried to discover the meaning of life and have come up with many answers, including many man-made religions and ideologies. But as we have seen, it is not there to be found, certainly not if we look for it under the sun – it is beyond us and far too deep. It appears this is one of the triggers for the Preacher as he sets out to know, to search and to seek out wisdom as to why things are as they are. It is a noble exercise and one to be commended but not if looking in the wrong places, as seen in previous chapters. He also wanted to identify evil and stupidity, foolishness and craziness, which come to think of it is also a worthwhile exercise because there is so much of it that is often accepted as part of life when it should be rather challenged, and is why wisdom is needed. Yesterday, we were reminded from Proverbs as to why wisdom is so important. So today, how about making: *"the fear of the Lord is the beginning of wisdom: and the knowledge of the holy is understanding"* Proverbs 9:10 our guiding principle and one that helps toward bringing meaning to life?

In rounding off this section, the Preacher rather bafflingly, at least for those living in a day when the equality of sexes is seen as important (and one we might want to take issue with), talks about the seductive, scheming of certain women who we (presumably if we are a man) do well to escape from (and can if we please God) and then goes on to say: *"I have looked for other answers but have found none. I found one man in a thousand that I could respect, but not one woman"* (7:28 GNT), and, putting aside the sex bias, he is saying that in effect there is a 0.05% chance of finding someone he could respect. He ends on a rather salutary note that pretty much sums up how he sees things, but it helps him to make at least some sense of the world: *"This is all that I have learned: God made us plain and simple, but we have made ourselves very complicated."* (7:28,29 GNT.) Maybe, we can learn from this the importance of having a simple trust in the Almighty.

Prayer: Lord, help us in our quest *to know, and to search, and to seek out wisdom, and the reason of things* and simply to trust in you, who does all things well. We thank you that in you and in following your ways we find true meaning to life.

Day 19: Being wise is a good thing (8:1)

"Who is as the wise man? and who knoweth the interpretation of a thing? a man's wisdom maketh his face to shine, and the boldness of his face shall be changed."

There is no doubt the Preacher thought wisdom was a good thing, even though he ended his life foolishly, like marrying foreign women who pressured him to turn from the Lord. At the start of his reign, it was wisdom that he wanted and asked God for, ahead of riches and power (a good example for us to follow), the getting of which is evidenced in his Books of Proverbs and Ecclesiastes, words which, as we have already said, were all about wisdom. He begins this part of his "sermon" by asking two pertinent questions, the answers to which we might all want to know. The desirability of being wise and knowing the right answers respectively, is also all too clear. Put in another way: *"only the wise know what things really mean. Wisdom makes them smile and makes their frowns disappear."* (8:1 GNT.)

Wisdom has practical, down to earth consequences, like submitting to authority, akin perhaps to honour thy father and mother. Here, it is about earthly authorities, *i.e.* kings: *"I counsel thee to keep the king's commandment, and that in regard of the oath of God. Be not hasty to go out of his sight: stand not in an evil thing; for he doeth whatsoever pleaseth him. Where the word of a king is, there is power: and who may say unto him, What doest thou?"* (8:2-4). Obedience to the ruler is an issue that faces us all and one Paul tried to tackle when writing to the church at Rome, then under the rule of a despotic Roman emperor: *"Let every soul be subject unto the higher powers. For there is no power but of God: the powers that be are ordained of God. Whosoever therefore resisteth the power, resisteth the ordinance of God"* Romans 13:1,2. The conclusion the Preacher comes to is to obey, although no doubt he would have recognised the times when not to, *e.g.* when it meant disobeying God. And he was quite clear that many kings were bad: *"I saw all this when I thought about the things that are done in this world, a world where some people have power and others have to suffer under them"* (8:9). But when it comes to getting a proper perspective on life and practising wisdom, the Preacher understood: *"There is a right time and a right way to do everything, but we know so little! None of us knows what is going to happen, and there is no one to tell us. No one can keep from dying or put off the day of death. That is a battle we cannot escape; we cannot cheat our way out* (8:6-8 GNT). Life's events are indeterminate, other than we die, even if we know little, including when we die. But there is a right time and way to do things, like seeking the way of wisdom.

Prayer: Forgive us Lord when we despise the way of wisdom, when knowing wisdom to be a good thing. Give us grace to submit to both good and bad kings.

Day 20: Fearing God is a good thing (8:12,13)

"Though a sinner do evil an hundred times, and his days be prolonged, yet surely I know that it shall be well with them that fear God, which fear before him: But it shall not be well with the wicked, neither shall he prolong his days, which are as a shadow; because he feareth not before God."

Life is unfair. We know, from earlier in his sermon, the Preacher was well aware when looking at life from the viewpoint of under the sun the wicked often appear to be better off than the righteous. His observations are quite salutary, insofar as when bad people die they are praised, despite their wrong doings, and people do wrong because they know they can get away with it: *"Yes, I have seen the wicked buried and in their graves, but on the way back from the cemetery people praise them in the very city where they did their evil. It is useless. Why do people commit crimes so readily? Because crime is not punished quickly enough"*. (8:10,11 GNT). Yet, according to our text, despite the injustice of it all and especially when taking the view of life beyond the sun, the wicked will get their comeuppance, one way or another (life really is that short) and because he does not fear God.

The Preacher reverts back to a notion he has promoted twice already, that is also considered in other places in scripture *e.g.*: *"Let us eat and drink; for tomorrow we shall die"* Isaiah 22:13; *"what advantageth it me, if the dead rise not? let us eat and drink; for tomorrow we die"* 1 Corinthians 15:32. For such is the consequence if there is no resurrection; but for the Preacher, the just and the wicked all ending in the same place – dead: *"There is a vanity which is done upon the earth; that there be just men, unto whom it happeneth according to the work of the wicked; again, there be wicked men, to whom it happeneth according to the work of the righteous: I said that this also is vanity. Then I commended mirth, because a man hath no better thing under the sun, than to eat, and to drink, and to be merry: for that shall abide with him of his labour the days of his life, which God giveth him under the sun"* (8:14,15).

But again, after he wrestles with these matters, he sees things a lot clearer and the way of wisdom comes out on top: *"When I applied mine heart to know wisdom, and to see the business that is done upon the earth: (for also there is that neither day nor night seeth sleep with his eyes:) Then I beheld all the work of God, that a man cannot find out the work that is done under the sun: because though a man labour to seek it out, yet he shall not find it; yea further; though a wise man think to know it, yet shall he not be able to find it"* (8:16,17).

Prayer: We thank you Lord the wisest man who ever lived struggled with the idea bad people get away with being BAD, but when he thought about it from your perspective, as the all-wise, just God, he realised it is always best to fear you.

Day 21: What we don't know (9:1)

"For all this I considered in my heart even to declare all this, that the righteous, and the wise, and their works, are in the hand of God: no man knoweth either love or hatred by all that is before them."

The Preacher returns to ideas already considered – we don't know what life has in store for us (how can we?). The good guys (the wise and righteous) don't always come out best and the bad guys (the foolish and wicked) do. But both share a common fate – death, and we have no idea when that happens. We are all in God's hands. It is worth pondering, what God has to say: *"All things come alike to all: there is one event to the righteous, and to the wicked; to the good and to the clean, and to the unclean; to him that sacrificeth, and to him that sacrificeth not: as is the good, so is the sinner; and he that sweareth, as he that feareth an oath. This is an evil among all things that are done under the sun, that there is one event unto all: yea, also the heart of the sons of men is full of evil, and madness is in their heart while they live, and after that they go to the dead. For to him that is joined to all the living there is hope: for a living dog is better than a dead lion. For the living know that they shall die: but the dead know not anything, neither have they any more a reward; for the memory of them is forgotten. Also their love, and their hatred, and their envy, is now perished; neither have they any more a portion for ever in anything that is done under the sun"* (9:2-6).

Yet there is a positive side to this rather gloomy commentary on life, and it relates to how we should live in the light of it. Firstly: enjoy life, recognising God is favourably inclined toward what we do: *"Go thy way, eat thy bread with joy, and drink thy wine with a merry heart; for God now accepteth thy works"* (9:7). Then how we dress (white garments), so be happy and cheerful: *"Let thy garments be always white; and let thy head lack no ointment"* (9:8). Then something really practical (to those of us so blessed) – enjoy life with the wife: *"Live joyfully with the wife whom thou lovest all the days of the life of thy vanity, which he hath given thee under the sun, all the days of thy vanity: for that is thy portion in this life, and in thy labour which thou takest under the sun"* (9:9). Then there is work, whether for a living, or to pursue some interest etc. While, from an under the sun perspective, there is no work once we die, it is worth doing well while we can: *"Whatsoever thy hand findeth to do, do it with thy might; for there is no work, nor device, nor knowledge, nor wisdom, in the grave, whither thou goest"* (9:10).

Prayer: We thank you Lord your word tells us what we need to know even if the raw truth can hurt. We thank you for good things you give us to enjoy and for the activities in life. May these be productive and may we do so as best we can.

Day 22: Time and chance (9:11,12)

"I returned, and saw under the sun, that the race is not to the swift, nor the battle to the strong, neither yet bread to the wise, nor yet riches to men of understanding, nor yet favour to men of skill; but time and chance happeneth to them all. For man also knoweth not his time: as the fishes that are taken in an evil net, and as the birds that are caught in the snare; so are the sons of men snared in an evil time, when it falleth suddenly upon them."

If we needed concrete examples of how life is unpredictable and unfair, today's text provides it (9:11). When we think about it, while exceptions to the rule do exist, there are many of them. The Preacher, as if to reinforce his point, then gives examples of how death or something disagreeable can befall us any time.

1. The fastest do not always win the race.
2. The strongest are not always the victors in battle.
3. The wise are not always rewarded with bread.
4. Those who understand are not necessarily rich.
5. The most skilled are not always granted favour.

In a world where we expect the best to be rewarded, over what is less than best, it should follow none of the above will happen. But not only is it something the Preacher had observed, it is likely we can all cite examples (likely many) of that being so and, moreover, there seems to be little we can do about it, much as we might want to, despite our best efforts or our cheering (or even praying) on the person who deserves to be rewarded. That is how life under the sun is and we find here the Preacher eloquently banging home the point he has been making throughout his sermon. Then to rub it in, he gives examples that irrespective of our best efforts, the worst can happen: *"Bad luck happens to everyone. You never know when your time is coming"* (9:11b,12a GNT). The examples are *"like birds suddenly caught in a trap"* and *"like fish caught in a net"* (both can happen at any time and neither the birds nor the fish can see what is coming), and so it is that *"we are trapped at some evil moment when we least expect it"* (9:12b GNT).

This might be a good juncture, if preaching the gospel, to point out life without God is meaningless because it is so unfair. We might reflect that often those who respond best to the gospel message are those who have been victims of injustices to be found in this world. But we can remind ourselves of the words of Jesus: *"I am come that they might have life, and that they might have it more abundantly"* John 10:10. Life under the sun is unfair, but God has something better in store.

Prayer: We are constantly bemused Lord at the uncertainties and unfairness of life, but are grateful that you have the answers. May we embrace your gift of life.

Day 23: Wisdom and foolishness contrasted (9:17,18)

"The words of wise men are heard in quiet more than the cry of him that ruleth among fools. Wisdom is better than weapons of war: but one sinner destroyeth much good."

"There is something else I saw, a good example of how wisdom is regarded in this world. There was a little town without many people in it. A powerful king attacked it. He surrounded it and prepared to break through the walls. Someone lived there who was poor, but so clever that he could have saved the town. But no one thought about him. I have always said that wisdom is better than strength, but no one thinks of the poor as wise or pays any attention to what they say. It is better to listen to the quiet words of someone wise than to the shouts of a ruler at a council of fools. Wisdom does more good than weapons, but one sinner can undo a lot of good." (9:13-18 GNT.)

Throughout the Book of Proverbs, the same preacher who wrote Ecclesiastes had been contrasting the way of wisdom with that of foolishness, affirming with many examples why the former is the way to go and in general things will go a lot better for the wise than the foolish. In Ecclesiastes, his emphasis changes due to his observations of life under the sun. Yet that same "Proverbs" consideration applies – in our verses today and in those in the next chapter. If there is a difference, it is the way that is *not* wisdom is not necessarily foolishness – who can argue with anyone wanting to defend his community against the attack, for example? Then the rewards of wisdom (harking back to yesterday's reflection) are not necessarily commensurate with what the wise person has achieved. Here we see a poor man saving his town from such an attack (we don't know how) through his wisdom, proving (perhaps) the point: *wisdom is better than strength,* yet that poor man was *not* rightly rewarded. One of the reasons is *no one thinks of the poor as wise or pays any attention to what they say.* From the Preacher's perspective, this is how wisdom is regarded in the world – the wise do not get their just desserts!

Yet this (presumably) now old man has not changed his mind from when he was (presumably) a lot younger and was setting out his many proverbs. Wisdom still is a good thing and is something worth pursuing. Firstly: *"The quiet words of the wise are more effective than the ranting of a king of fools"* (9:17 MSG). Secondly: *"Wisdom is better than warheads, but one hothead can ruin the good earth"* (9:18). If we are to contrast wisdom and foolishness, the advice given in all Solomon's writings always holds strong – we need to follow the way of wisdom.

Prayer: Thank you Lord for this timely reminder that the way of wisdom is the one we need to follow and the way of foolishness is the one we ought to avoid.

Day 24: Portrait of a fool (10:1)

"Dead flies cause the ointment of the apothecary to send forth a stinking savour: so doth a little folly him that is in reputation for wisdom and honour."

According to the KJV, the words "fool" or "folly" are used nine times in this Chapter (10), which is mainly about the way of wisdom as being the appropriate response to living life under the sun. The bottom line is foolishness can undo and undermine all the good that wisdom has achieved or might achieve in the future. *"Dead flies can make a whole bottle of perfume stink, and a little stupidity can cancel out the greatest wisdom. It is natural for the wise to do the right thing and for fools to do the wrong thing. Their stupidity will be evident even to strangers they meet along the way; they let everyone know that they are fools."* (10:1-3 GNT.) Dead flies in a bottle of ointment, presumably expensive and valued because of its fragrance etc., is a case of something to avoid – since all the good that may have been achieved through the application of wisdom is then undone – possibly in an instant. But we can all think of examples when this happens in real life. Similarly, we can see examples of wise people doing the right thing and fools doing the wrong, and seeing how people, who don't know who's who when meeting strangers, react accordingly to the wisdom and folly respectively that they may have seen – making it all too clear which side we ought to be on.

Before considering something ironic, notwithstanding the truth of the above, the Preacher offers some sound advice concerning life under the sun when he paints a scenario that we may well have experienced personally and why our keeping a cool head when under the proverbial cosh is good: *"If your ruler becomes angry with you, do not hand in your resignation; serious wrongs may be pardoned if you keep calm."* (10:4 GNT.) So back to our "wish you were kidding but I know you aren't" point and again something we may often observe – concerning those in government or running departments or whatever – those who are in charge may well be stupid people, and as for those who we may deem more worthy – they are often passed over. It is unjust, but then we are back to how life is under the sun: *"Here is an injustice I have seen in the world – an injustice caused by rulers. Stupid people are given positions of authority while the rich are ignored. I have seen slaves on horseback while noblemen go on foot like slaves."* (10:5-7 GNT.) If there is a lesson to learn, before we move on to more profound stuff to do with wisdom, it is that however unfair etc., life may be, given fools seem to prosper and are rewarded, it is still always well to be wise and that is how we should be.

Prayer: We thank you Lord for the reminder that a small amount of folly can undo the good achieved by a lot of wisdom. Preserve us from doing foolish acts, we pray, and even when we see fools prosper, may we choose to do what is right.

Day 25: Wise words that are gracious (10:12)

"The words of a wise man's mouth are gracious; but the lips of a fool will swallow up himself."

We will first look at some profound yet, when we think about it, sensible advice: *"Caution: The trap you set might catch you. Warning: Your accomplice in crime might double-cross you. Safety first: Quarrying stones is dangerous. Be alert: Felling trees is hazardous. Remember: The duller the axe the harder the work; Use your head: The more brains, the less muscle. If the snake bites before it's been charmed, What's the point in then sending for the charmer?"* (10:8-11 MSG.) When we think of traps that backfire – the Bible is full of examples, and like when wicked Haman built gallows to hang righteous Mordecai and ended up being hung on them himself. History is full of examples of criminals double crossed by their accomplices; we know occupations like quarrying stones and felling trees can be dangerous and those thus engaged need to take precautions; working with a blunt axe is a good example of spending needless effort that could have been avoided if the axe was sharp and as for snakes – the point about them biting before they have been charmed is noted. The moral is simple – "be wise!"

We return to wisdom and why it is superior to folly. *"The words of a wise person are gracious. The talk of a fool self-destructs – He starts out talking nonsense and ends up spouting insanity and evil. Fools talk way too much, chattering stuff they know nothing about. A decent day's work so fatigues fools that they can't find their way back to town."* (10:12-15 MSG.) It is a beautiful thought that is sometimes missed that when a wise person speaks, these are gracious words and how much these are welcomed and needed. It reminds us of when Jesus spoke at the synagogue in Nazareth: *"And all bare him witness, and wondered at the gracious words which proceeded out of his mouth. And they said, Is not this Joseph's son?"* Luke 4:22. The wisest person to have lived was ever gracious: *"A bruised reed shall he not break, and the smoking flax shall he not quench"* Isaiah 42:3 and *"The Lord God hath given me the tongue of the learned, that I should know how to speak a word in season to him that is weary"* Isaiah 50:4. How much the example of the wise contrasts with the empty words of the fool and not just words but their destructive whole way of life. The world is crying out for wise people and their gracious words, just as much as it cries out against foolish people and their *"mischievous madness"*. May we be found among the gracious wise.

Prayer: Dear Lord, we thank you for our Lord Jesus Christ who was all wise and ever gracious. We thank you for the timely reminder of the pitfalls of life and the need to take wise precautions. Help us as we make our words wise and gracious.

Day 26: Our attitude toward rulers (10:20)

"Curse not the king, no not in thy thought; and curse not the rich in thy bedchamber: for a bird of the air shall carry the voice, and that which hath wings shall tell the matter."

Today, we will consider kings or, our modern day near equivalent: those who rule over our lives. While we may accept this sobering fact of life with understandable reticence, given what we know about them, and however much we may want to qualify Paul's words, we ought to be mindful of the biblical injunction: *"Let every soul be subject unto the higher powers. For there is no power but of God: the powers that be are ordained of God. Whosoever therefore resisteth the power, resisteth the ordinance of God: and they that resist shall receive to themselves damnation. For rulers are not a terror to good works, but to the evil. Wilt thou then not be afraid of the power? do that which is good"* Romans 13:1-3, and act accordingly. Solomon aka "the Preacher" was a king and besides his great wisdom he also understood how "the system" worked and how best to work the system. A motley bunch, kings may be, but it is worth being reminded from his other book to do with wisdom that *"The king's heart is in the hand of the Lord, as the rivers of water: he turneth it whithersoever he will"* Proverbs 21:1.

Already in this chapter, we have been wowed by the thought *"If the spirit of the ruler rise up against thee, leave not thy place; for yielding pacifieth great offences"* (10:4) and alarmed at the notion that despite how egregious folly is, kings can and do exalt fools to positions of authority, who thus empowered go on to harm those who want to just get on with their lives. It may be a further reason for another of Paul's exhortations that: *"supplications, prayers, intercessions, and giving of thanks, be made for all men; for kings, and for all that are in authority; that we may lead a quiet and peaceable life in all godliness and honesty"* 1Timothy 2:1,2. It brings us to two more, pretty insightful, kingly texts. Firstly, a statement of fact: *"Woe to thee, O land, when thy king is a child, and thy princes eat in the morning! Blessed art thou, O land, when thy king is the son of nobles, and thy princes eat in due season, for strength, and not for drunkenness!"* (10:16,17). Secondly, some sound advice, which may help us to come to terms with living life that is conducted mostly under the sun: *"Curse not the king, no not in thy thought; and curse not the rich in thy bedchamber: for a bird of the air shall carry the voice, and that which hath wings shall tell the matter"* (10:20).

Prayer: Lord, we praise you that you raise up and put down kings, and you can since you are ruler over all the universe. Help us to conduct ourselves wisely when dealing with earthly authorities, who we pray for in your mighty Name.

Day 27: Casting our bread upon the waters (11:1)

"Cast thy bread upon the waters: for thou shalt find it after many days."

"Be generous: Invest in acts of charity. Charity yields high returns. Don't hoard your goods; spread them around. Be a blessing to others. This could be your last night. When the clouds are full of water, it rains. When the wind blows down a tree, it lies where it falls. Don't sit there watching the wind. Do your own work. Don't stare at the clouds. Get on with your life. Just as you'll never understand the mystery of life forming in a pregnant woman, So you'll never understand the mystery at work in all that God does. Go to work in the morning and stick to it until evening without watching the clock. You never know from moment to moment how your work will turn out in the end." (11:1-6 MSG.)

Anyone who has thrown bread upon water will likely have found it had dissipated after not too many minutes. Many modern paraphrase Bible versions will add their own interpretation of what the original language meant. From what we can make out, "casting our bread upon the waters" is tantamount to doing something good or taking a risk, usually without presuming very much in return. And if we do that and maybe buck the trend, rather than simply maintaining the status quo and finding all sorts of excuses to procrastinate or do little that truly matters, we will do something that truly makes a difference, even if we can't see how.

By way of elaboration, the Preacher makes sober observations and gives salutary advice on how we should conduct ourselves. As another paraphrase puts it: *"Put your investments in several places – many places even – because you never know what kind of bad luck you are going to have in this world"*. (11:2 GNT.) We are told not to hang around waiting for the perfect moment that may never come, because, using a farming metaphor, you will never plant anything and never harvest anything. Life is a mystery and none of us knows how things will turn out (harking back to an earlier observation). As for understanding, what better than the comparison with that of a baby developing in a mother's womb – we just don't know. We are encouraged simply to get to work regardless of external happenings and, to return to farming, we should sow in the evening as well as the morning, because we don't know which one, either or both, will yield the harvest. While there is a place for watching and dreaming (and of course praying, and not forgetting the need for wisdom), these are no excuse for putting off doing and the reason we do is so we can bless others. Be like great people of the past who did great good despite the obstacles, because they cast their bread upon the waters.

Prayer: Dear Lord, may we be those who cast our bread upon the waters. We thank you for the promise of a great return, even if figuring out how is beyond us.

Day 28: Life is a gift (11:9,10)

"Rejoice, O young man, in thy youth; and let thy heart cheer thee in the days of thy youth, and walk in the ways of thine heart, and in the sight of thine eyes: but know thou, that for all these things God will bring thee into judgment. Therefore remove sorrow from thy heart, and put away evil from thy flesh: for childhood and youth are vanity."

"It is good to be able to enjoy the pleasant light of day. Be grateful for every year you live. No matter how long you live, remember that you will be dead much longer. There is nothing at all to look forward to. Young people, enjoy your youth. Be happy while you are still young. Do what you want to do, and follow your heart's desire. But remember that God is going to judge you for whatever you do. Don't let anything worry you or cause you pain. You aren't going to be young very long." (11:7-11 GNT.)

Some of us can recall three-point sermons, with each point starting with the same letter of the alphabet. From the four verses that form our main text, we could make as our points: ***realistic, responsible*** and ***relevant***. The Preacher rarely disappoints in his ***realistic*** assessment of life under the sun. His ***responsible*** approach is commendable. His ***relevant*** observations of how things are, are noteworthy. He makes a point about the actuality of life and good things available to us, like the pleasant light of day and being able to enjoy the simple pleasures of life, which unlike most pleasures many seek after – are ***free***. He follows this up with something obvious – to take each day as it comes and treat it as a gift – bearing in mind there will be dark days too and the ending of all that is death.

Ecclesiastes is often seen as a book for older people. He returns to that audience in his next (final) chapter. Here he focuses on the young and aims his remarks at them. *"Young people, enjoy your youth. Be happy while you are still young. Do what you want to do, and follow your heart's desire"* is upbeat by any standard. There is wisdom drawing in the young, and "churches" have often prioritised their resources to do so, for most people who give their lives over to God do so when they are young. We may well ask why, but being less encumbered by the heavy weights of life or being beholden to prejudice and being set in one's ways are less likely to be barriers. But his counsel is to enjoy life while you are young, while you can, given you don't have the duties, burdens and physical and mental limitations of older people, and yet to maintain that responsible approach: *"But remember that God is going to judge you for whatever you do. Don't let anything worry you or cause you pain. You aren't going to be young very long"*.

Prayer: Thank you Lord for the gift of life. Please help us not to squander it.

Day 29: Remember God when you are young (12:1)

"Remember now thy Creator in the days of thy youth, while the evil days come not, nor the years draw nigh, when thou shalt say, I have no pleasure in them."

"*While the sun, or the light, or the moon, or the stars, be not darkened, nor the clouds return after the rain: In the day when the keepers of the house shall tremble, and the strong men shall bow themselves, and the grinders cease because they are few, and those that look out of the windows be darkened, And the doors shall be shut in the streets, when the sound of the grinding is low, and he shall rise up at the voice of the bird, and all the daughters of musick shall be brought low; Also when they shall be afraid of that which is high, and fears shall be in the way, and the almond tree shall flourish, and the grasshopper shall be a burden, and desire shall fail: because man goeth to his long home, and the mourners go about the streets: Or ever the silver cord be loosed, or the golden bowl be broken, or the pitcher be broken at the fountain, or the wheel broken at the cistern. Then shall the dust return to the earth as it was: and the spirit shall return unto God who gave it. Vanity of vanities, saith the preacher; all is vanity*" (12:2-8).

We continue where we left off yesterday, with the Preacher speaking to the youth his direct message of: "*Remember now thy Creator*". Being a wise man, and like many who are old, he saw what took place in the intervening years in his own life, having tried everything, concluding as he had begun: *Vanity of vanities, saith the preacher; all is vanity*. His rationale is one those of us who are old can identify with, looking back when we were young, with all our faculties, full of youthful energy and optimism, without the worries that came later to us: "*Before the years take their toll and your vigor wanes, Before your vision dims and the world blurs And the winter years keep you close to the fire. In old age, your body no longer serves you so well. Muscles slacken, grip weakens, joints stiffen. The shades are pulled down on the world. You can't come and go at will. Things grind to a halt. The hum of the household fades away. You are wakened now by bird-song. Hikes to the mountains are a thing of the past. Even a stroll down the road has its terrors. Your hair turns apple-blossom white, Adorning a fragile and impotent matchstick body. Yes, you're well on your way to eternal rest, While your friends make plans for your funeral*". (12:2-5 MSG.) Such beautiful yet haunting insights as he reflects on how life ends – willing for the young not to squander it (unlike he had) and to remember God: "*Life, lovely while it lasts, is soon over. Life as we know it, precious and beautiful, ends. The body is put back in the same ground it came from. The spirit returns to God, who first breathed it.*" (12:6-7 MSG.)

Prayer: Lord, we can think of young people who don't *remember their creator*. We pray for them and may we who are older be examples, living lives for you.

Day 30: The conclusion of the matter (12:9-11)

"And moreover, because the preacher was wise, he still taught the people knowledge; yea, he gave good heed, and sought out, and set in order many proverbs. The preacher sought to find out acceptable words: and that which was written was upright, even words of truth. The words of the wise are as goads, and as nails fastened by the masters of assemblies, which are given from one shepherd."

"Besides being wise himself, the Quester also taught others knowledge. He weighed, examined, and arranged many proverbs. The Quester did his best to find the right words and write the plain truth. The words of the wise prod us to live well. They're like nails hammered home, holding life together. They are given by God, the one Shepherd." (12:9-11 MSG.)

Now at the end of Ecclesiastes, the Preacher (Teacher, Philosopher, Quester) sums up. We will consider his conclusion in two parts – today and tomorrow, noting yesterday we left off where he began – life, lived out under the sun, is vanity – but there is hope if you bring God into the equation. He has already begun to do so and tomorrow we get the grand finale of what makes life meaningful. There is no false modesty here when the Preacher declares himself to be wise and one senses his sense of grave responsibility when he declares he has done his best to pass on the wisdom he has learned – not just because it was given to him by God but he has learned it the hard way. Having addressed our key thought yesterday of remembering our Creator when young and a lifetime of serving and enjoying God, we see him pass on a worthwhile legacy for those we leave behind. Here, the Preacher gives it his best shot (and we can do no better ourselves). The truth is the truth and his job was to present it as best he could in the realisation *"the sayings of the wise are like the sharp sticks that shepherds use to guide sheep, and collected proverbs are as lasting as firmly driven nails. They have been given by God, the one Shepherd of us all."* (12:11 GNT.) Besides passing on this whole truth matter (and often to do so comes at a personal cost – ridicule, rejection etc.) we must live it out – we are without excuse if we don't, because God is speaking to all of us concerning how we conduct ourselves when it comes to living life under and beyond the sun – and tomorrow we nail what exactly the Preacher says we need to do. As a final thought – it is a great privilege and responsibility to pass on what God is saying (word and deed). For those who do, wherever that is, it is not something to be treated lightly. We should honour those who do so well.

Prayer: We thank you Lord for the Preacher and his message of the vanity of life under the sun. We thank you too, you are in control – may we follow your way.

Day 31: The whole duty of man (12:12-14)

"And further, by these, my son, be admonished: of making many books there is no end; and much study is a weariness of the flesh. Let us hear the conclusion of the whole matter: Fear God, and keep his commandments: for this is the whole duty of man. For God shall bring every work into judgment, with every secret thing, whether it be good, or whether it be evil."

Before we conclude, a word needs saying about books. The Preacher comes across as a breath of fresh air, especially to book lovers, for he was widely read and books played a vital part in his understanding of the world. But there are limits, as he explained – having studied a lot of what went on in the world, he concluded it was chasing the wind. Now he adds that there is no end to doing such studies, which *is a weariness of the flesh*. He ends advising us on what we need to do, and it is straightforward and simple, if we have the resolve so to do: *Fear God, and keep his commandments: for this is the whole duty of man*. In our earlier study on Proverbs, we reflected upon an important point: the fear of the Lord. Years on, we see Solomon has not changed his mind. We saw from the original language that fear covered a wide spectrum from respect to dread. While YHWH God is portrayed, even in the OT, as a loving father and husband, he is also someone to be feared and this is best encapsulated in the notions of awe and reverence. Fear, sadly, at least for things or rather the One that matters, is often missing in today's culture, including those who profess belief in God. Yet fearing God is mentioned twice as many times as loving and trusting God combined, in both OT and NT, and for the Preacher it is the very thing that is needed for living life that to many can only be viewed as under the sun, but to those who believe needs to be lived in the light of what is beyond the sun – in accordance with God's commands, which we are required to keep. While, as believers in the saving grace of the Lord Jesus Christ, we have confidence on the Day of Judgement, not in our good works but rather in His finished work, the Preacher's final words are a sober reminder of why we should fear God: *For God shall bring every work into judgment, with every secret thing, whether it be good, or whether it be evil*. We can easily pass ourselves off as righteous etc., but God is able to judge our motives and actions and can see things about us that no-one else sees. And while these thoughts are sobering, they are also thrilling, because life now has meaning and we have purpose, despite life's vanity and much chasing after the wind. Even so, we will, as we always have, experience both good and bad in life (we are not immune), but our marching orders are clear, *i.e.: Fear God, and keep his commandments!*

Prayer: Dear Lord, we thank you for the many amazing lessons we have learned from Ecclesiastes. May we be those who fear you and keep your commandments.

Education from Ecclesiastes

When I set out to study Ecclesiastes in preparation for this book, I was fairly clear that whereas Song of Songs was geared more for the young with its message of love, and Proverbs was more for the middle aged with its message of wisdom, Ecclesiastes was likely to appeal more to the elderly with its sober observations concerning the vanity of life and its uncertainties, just as applicable for those who resolve to follow the ways of love and wisdom. It is not quite as simple as that (it rarely is) for there is content in each of Solomon's books pertinent for all ages.

Following my most recent studies, the further thought occurred to me that the Song of Songs is a book for the optimist, since we can always hold on to the thought that love triumphs over everything, especially death; Proverbs is a book for the realist since, given that if we were to follow the way of wisdom it sets out, life will go well for us, with the corollary being life will not go well if we do not follow the way of wisdom. When we come to Ecclesiastes, while there is no dispute the ways of love and wisdom are the ones we ought to follow (after all it was the same author in each), but even if we do, life may not turn out as well as one might hope or deserve. The big factor is earthly inhabitant "players" in world events, in the main, live life under the sun and follow a way described as vanity, and then there are the unseen non-earthly players, whose ways are unfathomable.

The beauty of Ecclesiastes is that despite its more pessimistic outlook on life, there is more than a modicum of hope and in fact, because it sets out, possibly better than anywhere in Holy Scripture, how things really are down here on earth, it provides a solid framework for coming to terms with life under the sun and how we should conduct ourselves amidst the uncertainties of life. It provides unique insights on how to go about our daily business and make sense of our environment and those activities that humanity may consider important, noting its author had tried them all and, to use his own word, found that all were vanity (meaningless). Because that is how life is and the brutal fact is most people operate in a paradigm of vanity, we can have a measure of calm assurance, knowing God is in control.

Without giving the answer (it is not 42 for "Hitchhikers to the Galaxy" fans), the Preacher (Solomon) has a fair crack at answering the question that has been asked since the beginning of time: by those wanting to find the answer to life, the universe, everything. Having set out his stall at the start: "*Vanity of vanities, saith the Preacher, vanity of vanities; all is vanity*" (1:2) he tells his readers what they need to do at the end: "*Fear God, and keep his commandments: for this is the whole duty of man*" (12:13), while leaving everything open such that people have a measure of freedom to act according to their circumstances, interests etc.

While Ecclesiastes is full of gems that for many are untapped (and is worth studying for that reason alone – and it comprises only twelve not all that long chapters), it is a book suited as much for the irreligious as the religious, especially those with an enquiring mind. It dispenses with pious platitudes and does not beat around the bush and is pretty down to earth in saying what needs to be said. As such, it is an ideal book to wake people up regarding how things really are and how they stand in the eternal and universal scheme of things. While God is brought into "the sermon", Solomon does not overdo it, making common sense observations that even unbelievers would find themselves hard put to dispute.

In a way that might seem odd to some, as we begin to dig beneath the surface in Ecclesiastes, there is a lot there to be discovered that can bring us comfort. There is no doubt that seriously following the Lord can often be a lonely undertaking, as we refuse to go along with what we are told and one that can bring us pain and ridicule, just as darkness recoils from the light. Often our God given insights are not taken to much by a world that rejects God and refuses to follow His ways and in doing so reject those who follow His ways. But in reading through Ecclesiastes, we know why, if we didn't know before – for those who live life as under the sun leave too little room for life beyond the sun. This is not to make us feel better necessarily or cause us to be complacent, but rather it gives us the serenity to accept that is how things are. For God followers, it is back to Ecclesiastes 12:13.

Solomon, in wisely analysing much of human activity, often from the perspective of having had first-hand experience and insider insights, has provided much that is of value, made even more credible because of his wisdom and experience. In my own attempts at sharing the gospel message (something all Christian believers are required to do – one way or another), I might now be inclined to first present the teachings of Ecclesiastes, not just to highlight how life is when it is lived out as under the sun, but how life is when God is left out. Then I would present the teachings of one or other of the Gospels, with their message of hope and salvation, which tells us how life can and should be lived, with God central to the picture.

It is fitting that in winding up our analysis (excuse the term) of Solomon's three Bible books, that we end on a note that is to do with the *whole duty of man*. It is this author's prayer that readers recognise what that duty is and they go and do it.

Quoting from Ecclesiastes

When it comes to memorable Bible quotes, we are spoiled for choice, and nowhere more so than in the Book of Ecclesiastes. I offer here my 20 favourites (from the NIV). Maybe you can add your own:

""Meaningless! Meaningless!" says the Teacher. "Utterly meaningless! Everything is meaningless."" (1:2).

"What has been will be again, what has been done will be done again; there is nothing new under the sun" (1:9).

"Is there anything of which one can say, "Look! This is something new"? It was here already, long ago; it was here before our time" (1:10).

"There is no remembrance of people of old, and even those who are yet to come will not be remembered by those who follow them" (1:11).

"I applied my mind to study and to explore by wisdom all that is done under the heavens. What a heavy burden God has laid on the human race!" (1:13).

"There is a time for everything, and a season for every activity under the heavens" (3:1).

"A time to tear and a time to mend, a time to be silent and a time to speak" (3:7).

"He has made everything beautiful in its time. He has also set eternity in the human heart; yet no one can fathom what God has done from beginning to end" (3:11).

"Two are better than one, because they have a good return for their labor" (4:9).

"Guard your steps when you go to the house of God. Go near to listen rather than to offer the sacrifice of fools, who do not know that they do wrong" (5:1).

"A good name is better than fine perfume, and the day of death better than the day of birth" (7:1).

"Do not say, "Why were the old days better than these?" For it is not wise to ask such questions" (7:10).

"Whatever your hand finds to do, do it with all your might, for in the realm of the dead, where you are going, there is neither working nor planning nor knowledge nor wisdom" (9:10).

"I have seen something else under the sun: The race is not to the swift or the battle to the strong, nor does food come to the wise or wealth to the brilliant or favor to the learned; but time and chance happen to them all" (9:11).

"As dead flies give perfume a bad smell, so a little folly outweighs wisdom and honor" (10:1).

"Sow your seed in the morning, and at evening let your hands not be idle, for you do not know which will succeed, whether this or that, or whether both will do equally well" (11:6).

"Remember your Creator in the days of your youth, before the days of trouble come and the years approach when you will say, "I find no pleasure in them"" (12:1).

"Be warned, my son, of anything in addition to them. Of making many books there is no end, and much study wearies the body" (12:12).

"Now all has been heard; here is the conclusion of the matter: Fear God and keep his commandments, for this is the duty of every human being" (12:13).

"For God will bring every deed into judgment, including every hidden thing, whether it is good or evil" (12:14).

Prophets Priests Kings and Jesus

Prior to writing this book, the author wrote *Prophets of the Bible*, an electronic version of which, alongside many of his other writings, including nearly 2000 blog articles, can be freely downloaded from his website: *jrbpublications.com*. The book attempted to cover the lives, ministries and times of all the Bible prophets; some well-known, some less known or unnamed and some not commonly regarded as prophets yet spoke or acted prophetically. It also covers the background and context in which prophets operated and issues raised when studying them, including end times prophecy and modern-day prophets, and covers in-depth most of the Bible. Paper copies of Prophets of the Bible (now second edition), alongside this book, is available via the Internet, e.g. Ingram and Amazon.

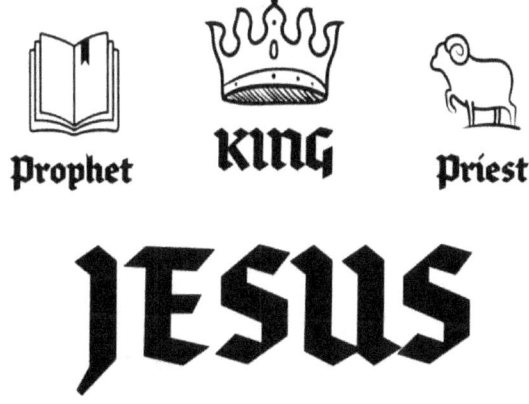

The author is currently working on a sequel to *Prophets of the Bible*, to be titled Kings and Priests of the Bible, which he intends to be available around the end of 2021. He will adopt much the same approach as he had with *Prophets of the Bible* but will minimise the repeating of content to do with context etc., even if relevant to each of prophets, priests and kings. It has been said that at different times in Israel's history, prophets, priests and kings (as well as the Patriarchs: Abraham, Isaac and Jacob (to which we might also add Joseph)) played dominant roles, often operating in tandem:

- 500 years – Abraham to the Exodus – Patriarchs
- 500 years – Exodus to Saul – Prophets
- 500 years – Saul to Exile – Kings
- 500 years – Exile to Jesus – Priests

Leadership under any of these offices was not entirely satisfactory, until Jesus came, who combined all these functions, yet who most of Israel rejected, but will return to planet earth as their promised Messiah. As far as this author is concerned, the Bible is principally about God (Father, Son and Holy Spirit) and His dealings with humankind, begging the question: how do we respond? "We", it should be added, includes both Jew and Gentile, bearing in mind God has ever sought a people who have a heart for Him alone. As interesting and instructive as the lives of prophets, priests and kings are, the Bible usually only tells us what God considers important, often leaving wide gaps in our knowledge.

If there is a focal point in the Bible narrative, bearing in mind a large portion of the afore-mentioned two books make reference to the Old Testament, when most of the Bible prophets, priests and kings operated, it is Jesus: prophet, priest and king, who stands head and shoulders over all other prophets, priests and kings, that for Christians is also their Lord and Saviour, and who we must keep our eyes fixed on. As for OT and NT; the OT, dominated by prophets, priests and kings, pointed readers toward Jesus' coming, and the NT was a fulfilment of what the OT, from the outset, was looking forward to.

www.ingramcontent.com/pod-product-compliance
Lightning Source LLC
Chambersburg PA
CBHW071926290426
44110CB00013B/1495